ACADEMIA LUNARE

Friendship in
The Lord of the Rings

Cristina Casagrande

Translated by
Eduardo Boheme

Academia
Lunare
LUNA PRESS
PUBLISHING

www.lunapresspublishing.com

ISBN-13: 978-1-913387-93-8

To Francisco,
Who was born alongside this project,
and now grows beautifully with it.

Contents

Seed-gift

Cesar Machado[1]

The trees were among Professor Tolkien's greatest loves. I cannot say whether this was an echo of his idyllic childhood, warm in his mother's arms, or only a form of love that grew naturally in his heart throughout his life. The only certainty is that, within his *legendarium* (the word that describes his vast mythology), these living beings play an irreplaceable role. Some of them can even talk and walk!

In particular, the *mallorn* ("golden tree" in the Elvish tongue) always seemed to me the most significant tree regarding friendship. Coming from the Blessed Realm of the angels it was taken, as a token of friendship, to an island inhabited by the highest Men that have ever lived. There, the *mallorn* grew even taller and more beautiful, perhaps because it was the offspring of a pure gift, in every sense of the word, seeking only the embellishment of someone else's life.

Thus, the *mallorn* became the most beloved among the trees in the Land of Gift, one of the island's many names, and its felling was forbidden by the kings of those proud men. Still in the times of wisdom and vigour, one of their sailor princes crossed the ocean and, as a gift to the last of the great Elven kings, he offered seeds of the golden tree. The friendship between the young prince of Men and the ancient Elven king was prosperous, even though the beautiful plant did not thrive in that new land.

Capriciously, its seeds preferred once again to serve as a gift between friendly peoples. They travelled for many months and miles in the hands of a noble Elven lady until they came to

1. Co-founder and host of the *Tolkien Talk* YouTube Channel.

a place where sadness had taken root. There, seeing that their poetry and light were necessary, they conversed with the earth, nourishing it. After some time, their green-, silver-, and gold-mixed leaves stretched their arms towards the skies and filled the place with dreams.

For thousands of years, their splendour and glory pulsed in that land, and there came a time when, heeding a last call of friendship, one single seed was assigned the mission of accompanying a simple gardener in a desperate journey. Small in size, but with a titanic braveness, its guardian grew valiantly in a barren, waterless land, facing deprivation and the absence of sunlight, with the one hope of returning to his sweet garden one day.

Once the seemingly impossible quest was fulfilled, the seed, as though nourished by the strength of its bearer, decided to sprout forth in the land it had once rejected. And to this day, thousands of years later, it remains, sublime in its beauty, in the place where its honourable protector planted it: in the heart of the Shire and of those who love true things.

Friendship is just like that: it picks the right moment and grows in accordance with the weather we provide it. Tolkien made the seed bloom from the angels to the Elves, and from them to Men and, lastly, to the small and humble. He always knew that books and trees alike are made of leaves and dreams.

Foreword - Fantasy Friend

Ronald Kyrmse[1]

J.R.R. Tolkien has been called "the author of the 20th century". Indeed, in English-speaking countries, the sales of *The Lord of the Rings* are surpassed only by those of the Bible. The extreme popularity of this imaginary-world creator — who influenced almost all authors of fantastic fiction since the 1950s — comes in great measure from the verisimilitude of his universe, so different from our own that we can, as it were, go there on vacation as we read. At the same time, it is so similar to our own that we can apply its message and lessons to our own lives. Thus, the Secondary World, product of subcreation — in Tolkien's terminology, the invention of a world by an author, who is, in turn, also created — is at once a reflection and a guide to the primary world we live in.

Tolkien's epic work shows us much about human relations: persistence, humility, nobility. Among them, friendship is certainly one of the most sought for and satisfying. Indeed, the very outcome of *The Lord of the Rings*, with fundamental consequences for Men's history (as narrated by Tolkien), depends to a great extent on the practice of friendship. This book shows not only how, but also why it was this way.

The appreciation of Tolkien's works started long before the highly popular films by Peter Jackson, which brought crowds of people to the movie theatres and generated legions of fans in the beginning of this century. However, it is important to note that, long before, groups could be found that aimed

---

1. Ronald Kyrmse has translated the majority of Tolkien's works in Brazil, including *The Lord of the Rings* (HaperCollins Brasil, 2019), and, in 2003, published his own book of essays, *Explicando Tolkien* [Explaining Tolkien] (Martins Fontes, 2003).

at studying seriously the subcreated world, deepening the knowledge about Tolkien's geography, his languages, his societies, and psychology, exploring them with the rigour of the so-called "serious" disciplines and with the academic prestige that fantasy cannot normally boast of, not even in Literary studies. In Brazil, such groups date back at least to the 1980s, being initially quite informal, and becoming gradually more organised, partly because of the positive potentialities of the internet.

Cristina Casagrande has the advantage of belonging simultaneously in the academic environment, bringing along the rigour of research, and the enthusiast field — the "Tolkienists" — employing to the study of the author, whom they call "the Professor", such energy that occasionally consumes time that "should" be employed to more serious tasks. But this amount of time is justifiably spent, for Tolkien himself often worked long into the night to elaborate his world when he could be delving deeper into the study of Anglo-Saxon language and literature instead.

Thus, while studying hundreds of pages and hours of movies — the same story told by two different bards — Cristina is able to show us the huge importance of friendship, a feeling that motivates us, conducts us, and, often, leads us to success. And which sees far, because it stands (as Newton's quote goes) on the shoulders of giants. Aristotle, Thomas Aquinas, and Tolkien saw human beings and their emotions clearly. Cristina Casagrande, in this work, evidences their view for our own understanding.

Preface

In mid-2011 I was newly-married and had just lost my job —
exactly 22 days before my wedding — and I was in my parents'
house trying to build up a strategic plan about what to do with
my career after that unexpected misfortune. My mother had
always encouraged me to pursue a master's degree but, having
two bachelor's degrees already, my mind was more bent on
working, making money, and finally getting rich — the last
part was a joke, but that would not be a bad idea.

Since my mother has always been my greatest example for
almost everything in life, I decided, at last, to follow her advice.
Pondering about what I could do really well, I reflected on what
touched my soul the deepest, and thought that would be half
the battle of contributing, even though minimally, to a slightly
better world. And so I came across the book *Educar para a
Amizade* [Educate for Friendship], by Gerardo Castillo,[1] which
was gathering dust on the shelf, trying to tell me something.

With a degree in Journalism and another one in Language
and Literature, I considered the latter to be more suited for
a master's degree *stricto sensu*,[2] since I had always left my
practical side to Journalism. I intended to take up something in
the area of Children's and Youth Literature, because the world
of the little ones always fascinated me, typical of someone who
had a very happy childhood. The title of that book attracted
me, and I started reflecting more on the matter: if people had
friendship as the foundation of their lives, much evil in the
world would attenuate — in the narrow and broad senses —
there would not be so much disloyalty, nor so much violence
and perversion, not even corruption or wars.

1. Castillo, Gerardo. *Educar para a amizade*. São Paulo: Quadrante, 1999.
2. In Brazil, a *stricto sensu* post-graduate course normally takes two years and has
a more academic bent than a *latu sensu* course.

I knew, of course, that I could not change the world but, since I would be spending the following years of my life mulling over the same subject, the ideal outcome was to give birth to this predicted eucatastrophe. I therefore started looking for professors at the University of São Paulo, where I had graduated, who could supervise projects in the area of Children's and Youth Literature. I then found professor Maria Zilda da Cunha, who generously welcomed me.

In the beginning, I had a mind to work with something more canonical for university standards and delved into the universe of *Sítio do Pica Pau Amarelo*,[3] and learned much about the great writer Monteiro Lobato. I took up some modules as a guest student and wrote two monographs, one of them about the Saci.[4] Imagine that: a monograph on friendship according to Aristotle, having Lobato's Saci as object. The result was not bad, but I realised that this mixture was not what I was looking for.

In a way, *The Lord of the Rings* had always been among my research goals, but I did not yet possess that characteristic of Tolkienian heroes: courage. To quote Tolkien, "let the psychoanalysts note!".[5] First, I considered the Oxford Professor's work too vast, deep, and complex. Additionally, I had to face the most conservative literary critics who claim, up to this day, that Tolkien is not literature, and prove to everyone that my choice was not merely a fan thing.

I have always been a great admirer of J.R.R. Tolkien's but was far from being an aficionado. I always felt small beside him, and my critical attitude would never let me conduct any academic study or professional work out of fanaticism. What attracted me was the feeling of being in good hands — Tolkien

---

3. Literally *Yellow Woodpecker Farm*, it is a series of children's books by the Brazilian author Monteiro Lobato (1882-1948). They are among the best-known children's books in the country.
4. "Saci" is a character from the Brazilian folklore who is also present in *Sítio do Pica Pau Amarelo*.
5. Tolkien, J.R.R., Carpenter, H. (Org.), Tolkien, C. (Assist.). *The Letters of J.R.R. Tolkien*. London: HarperCollins, 2006, Letter 180, p. 232.

and I share the same Christian ideals but, at the same time, he spoke to every kind of reader, from practicing Catholics to staunch atheists. He brought in his literature an extremely seductive universality, and I knew I could trust him. But, at the same time, I thought: "What about all those details? Look how critical and demanding his readers are! There is a new book coming out every day. Was it not only *The Hobbit* and *The Lord of the Rings* and, at most, *The Silmarillion*? Why on earth do they waste so much time discussing whether these fire dragons — I meant *Balrogs* — have wings or not?"

You might be a little curious to know how I first met Tolkien's works, and I regret to say that I cannot remember it well. I spent my adolescence attending a centre for Catholic education and confessed weekly to the same priest. He was very intelligent, liked very much to read, and in his lectures he frequently talked about *The Lord of the Rings*, always with sparkling eyes — I am almost sure that it was in one of these occasions that I first heard the name of the Professor, that is, J.R.R. Tolkien.

Also, with the same group of people, I worked as a volunteer during term, weekends, and during the winter and summer vacations, always somewhere in the countryside of São Paulo. In one of these trips, I met a girl who was a circus artist and who also worked as a volunteer. I thought she was incredible, being an artist, cool, free, and... she liked Tolkien's books! Nothing in her resembled the stereotype we usually have in mind of a *Lord of the Rings* aficionado. She sat in a circle with other girls telling the adventures of Bilbo and Frodo in the late afternoons after work. That was fascinating to me. How did she manage to read everything in one week? I wanted such an experience. But, however tempting, I chose not to listen to her storytelling, because I wanted to live that experience too. I wanted to get to know that book.

My first contact with the Tolkienian universe is a little different from the frequent clichés: someone who is very fond of fantastic stories, who went to the movies and loved

Peter Jackson's films and, afterwards, devoured the books. I met Tolkien through stories told orally by a priest and a circus acrobat. Thus, the stories of the Middle-earth had for me, since the beginning, a dash of magic — at least that is how it is imprinted in my memory — that took me to a spiritual plane and, at the same time, brought the beauty of art. And it continues to be like that.

Around the time Peter Jackson's movies were released, I asked my father to give me *The Lord of the Rings* as a birthday present. In the one-volume edition, I progressed until I reached the middle of *The Two Towers* but, after that, I stopped. It took me several years to read the entire novel, from the Shire to the appendices. Nowadays I know exactly why: I am quite prepared to start and finish but going through the shadowy winter of the middle is something I am still learning, and Tolkien has been helping me very much with that.

After two years thinking over the idea, I started my master's course in January 2014. I had been married for two years and had just had my son Francisco — much beloved and desired. And so, I started taking care of the twins — Francisco and master's degree — and to this day I do not know which one gives me harder work, but both give me much more happiness (Francisco of course wins that).

Despite being much more focused than most post-graduate candidates in my area, my pre-project was much different than the result. I had a very inchoate, even immature, idea of everything. I had a mind to study only the relation between the pairs of friends Merry and Pippin, Sam and Frodo, Legolas and Gimli etc.

At that point, I had already read *The Hobbit*, *The Silmarillion*, and two or three times *The Lord of the Rings*, including the original one in English. But that is far too little for a Tolkienist. It meant that the level of my research was quite elementary, and I had to work hard to deal with all that reading and rereading and meet the deadlines. Besides that, I had to plunge in the universe of comparative literature, intersemiotic studies of literature and cinema; the thought-provoking and challenging pages of Aristotle's *Nicomachean Ethics*, Thomas Aquinas's *Summa Theologiae*, and so forth.

With Aristotle, I learned that friendship was a virtue, or implied a virtue, which had a direct relationship with our concept of happiness. I also learned that such happiness as the ancients regarded it had a correspondence with the happy ending in fairy-stories, the "eucatastrophe", in Tolkienian terminology.

I learned with Thomas Aquinas that theological friendship imparts greater volume, weight, and flavour to this kind of relationship, and that reciprocity, so necessary between friends, can be filled by the communion with God. I also realised, through Aquinas, that the most perfect form of friendship lies in charity, and that it requires mercy: the trump card against the Enemy in the War of the Ring — Sauron and the very shadows that the heroes themselves bear.

I got to know closely every hero of the story and understood why it would not be possible to have a single character worthy of bearing alone this title, and how friendship grew stronger because of that. I realised that, just as it happens in our Primary World, each hero has a different personal journey and yet, through friendship, they can fight together for the same ideal.

Along the way, I experienced many victories and some defeats too. I had to pull myself together after the notorious phase of the proposal defence, and then had to find out how I would manage everything the best possible way in the final stretch. I could rely on my supervisor's huge patience and was lucky enough to be helped by one of the board examiners, Professor Diego Klautau.

Towards the end, I had the pleasure of meeting Cesar Machado and Sérgio Ramos, hosts of the Tolkien Talk YouTube Channel which, back then, was still in the beginning. I learned the ropes with them, and, as much as possible, all the rationale behind that vast and rich legendarium.

I was also very glad to be introduced to Ronald Kyrmse,

who wrote the foreword to this book. With him, I learned to care even more about words, feel the weight of responsibility in a translation, and be even more diligent while writing a text. With these three, thus, I learned to be a Tolkienist.

After the defence, I reaped the harvest of so much effort, of so many "noes" I had given to myself and to many opportunities in favour of a single project. Not few were the good and true friends I made — some of my greatest treasures — not to mention my personal and professional development.

The board of examiners suggested the publication of my master's thesis and, much to my delight, I was welcomed at Martin Claret Publishers. Publishing this book means the realization of a dream. Somehow, it is as though the Primary and Secondary Worlds collided, and gratitude is the unavoidable consequence.

Throughout these pages, I invite you to look closer at the heroes of *The Lord of the Rings*, to listen to the Ancients' wise voices — just like someone who is willing to heed Gandalf's advice — to reflect, and to be moved by new discoveries perhaps. I shall consider this Quest fulfilled if I learn that these pages transformed you on the inside and that, since then, you were never the same. But always in good company.

Chapter One

Nice to meet you. A brief introduction

"Certainly I looked for no such friendship as you have shown. To have found it turns evil to great good."[1] Those are Frodo Baggins's words to Faramir, Captain of Gondor, in the course of the gentle Hobbit's important mission to save his people and his friends from the power of Sauron, also known as the Enemy. In this simple sentence, Frodo shows that the bonds between two friends can be not only the solution to many problems, but the motivation behind many of the sacrifices we make throughout our lives.

Friendship in John Ronald Reuel Tolkien's (1892–1973) stories is not a rare theme. Far from it: we dare say it is the necessary condition for the plot to unfold. In the most important work published during his life, *The Lord of the Rings* (1954–1955), we find plenty of evidence, from the most obvious to the simplest, to prove that. An apparently unpretentious visit to an old farmer's house, or the brief company of a friendly Hobbit may not attract much attention within the plot, but they certainly help the narrative development.

To vanquish the evil power of the One Ring, beings of Middle-earth unite in a fellowship to oppose the Enemy, thus highlighting the strength of friendship not only by its presence, but also by its absence, when a character turns to evil and becomes, therefore, an enemy.

One finds the stamp of friendship in several examples with distinct configurations: the friendship between a supernatural and a human being, between people with historical feuds, between wholly different peoples, between individuals with

1. Tolkien, J.R.R. *The Lord of the Rings*. London: HarperCollins, 2008, p. 909.

distinct hierarchical positions, and so forth. Gandalf, the wizard, is called "best of friends" by Frodo and, because of this friendship, a relationship of trust is established between them, which prompts *The Hobbit* to accept his mission of bearer of the Ring. Gimli, the Dwarf and Legolas, the Elf, overcame the past disagreements between their peoples in favour of a greater, and shared, good, and they went beyond it: they became great friends. The realms of Rohan and Gondor united in friendship to fight against the Enemy. Frodo and his gardener, Sam, got even closer, setting aside their hierarchical distance through their virtuous dispositions and, together, they were able to reach the fire of Mordor, where the Ring would be destroyed.

Leaning over this theme, one realises that friendship does not contribute solely to the narrative development, but also to the inner growth of each character and to the decentralization of protagonism. Moreover, friendship is the essential condition for the heroes to reach their greatest objectives throughout their adventure.

Encouraged by the Middle-earth stories

J.R.R. Tolkien did not intend to be a famous author. His literary production sprang out of his innermost richness, that of one who loved languages, mythology, fairy-stories, the Primary World, and the Enchanted Realm. And he would always go beyond. A passionate soul that abandoned himself enthusiastically to what charmed him. Only then did he get to know closer and deeper that which fascinated him and which came to be his own literature.

Tolkien has a vast mythological and literary production,[2] based upon decades of research on philology, Germanic

---

2. The author created a fictional world based upon Germanic mythologies with the initial purpose of building a mythology for his country, England, which lacked such a body of works. This phenomenon is called "mythopoeia", mythmaking. Even though his overarching objective was to entertain his audience, *The Hobbit,* and mainly *The Lord of the Rings* were born out of this project which, to a greater extent, can be found in *The Silmarillion*, posthumously published.

mythology, the Middle Ages, and so forth. The greater part of his production served as a background for his two main works published during his life, *The Hobbit* and *The Lord of the Rings*. These studies were also used as a means of personal amusement, because his research was not always done with a view to publication and, the more he took pains to undertake research, so much more pleasure did he get from it.

His official biography tells us that the Oxford Professor once found a blank sheet among the exams he was correcting. He declares:

> "One of the candidates had mercifully left one of the pages with no writing on it [...] and I wrote on it: '*In a hole in the ground there lived a hobbit*'. Names always generate a story in my mind. Eventually I thought I'd better find out what hobbits were like. But that's only the beginning."[3]

The Professor, as he is known, first wrote *The Hobbit* as a story to be told to his young children, but the typescript ended up in Susan Dagnall's hands, then part of the staff at George Allen & Unwin publishing house. She persuaded Tolkien to send his story and try to publish it. After the great success of Bilbo Baggins's saga, the publishing house asked for a new work, a continuation of that book.

A curious fact is that Tolkien did not want to continue the adventure of *There and Back Again*,[4] because he was busy with the stories we now find in *The Silmarillion*, and which comprise mythological adventures that have more to do with the Elvish people. But the publishing house insisted in their initial bet and, thus, the writer started *The Lord of the Rings*, a novel with more than one thousand pages, which was published almost twenty years after he started it.[5]

---

3. Carpenter, H. *J.R.R. Tolkien: a Biography*. London: HarperCollins, 2002, p. 230.
4. The subtitle of *The Hobbit*.
5. Tolkien wanted to publish *The Silmarillion* along with *The Lord of the Rings*, but the economic problems after the War, such as costly paper, prompted the publishing houses to deny his request.

The largest work published during Tolkien's life, *The Lord of the Rings* tells the story of a magical ring, forged by Sauron, also known as the Dark Lord, who wants to conquer the whole Middle-earth by using the strong power of the Ring, capable of seducing and controlling whoever bore it. Frodo, a simple Hobbit from the Shire, was chosen among his friends to destroy the One Ring and, thus, bring back peace and safety for all the peoples of Middle-earth. The story was and still is a success that charms many readers worldwide.

The definition of the classics

Tolkien's studies about imagination were propped up against classical and medieval philosophy. Besides that, we understand that classical thought is the matrix of Western ethics and imagination, and that it continues to influence our comprehension of the world to this day. Therefore, the theoretical basis for the present reflection on friendship will be Aristotle's *Nicomachean Ethics*, since one can detect in the classical text a comprehensive and deep study about the theme.

The Nicomachean Ethics deals with nothing less than the greater good we all desire: happiness. The matter is simple and complex at the same time: the book brings up an examination of human behaviour, based on practical reason, aiming to achieve the ultimate good, that which requires no other good besides itself, because it suffices.

We could think of practical examples from our daily lives. Why do we brush our teeth? To achieve greater benefits, such as the pleasant sensation of a clean mouth, to avoid bad breath, to prevent bacterial infections, avoiding calculus and decay etc. Why do we study? To be admitted in a good university, to acquire knowledge, to secure a good job, and so on. Why do we want happiness? Because happiness suffices, it is our ultimate good, we want to brush our teeth and study because we want to be happy — in other words, to feel fulfilled, which is synonymous to that state of being.

Such an ultimate good has a Greek name, *eudaimonia*, which is commonly translated and perceived as happiness. Roberto Catunda's[6] explanation can help us understand this concept further:

> The realization of *eudaimonia* is described by Aristotle as an action of the soul according to excellence (arete). Thus, it is necessary to know what soul and excellence are, so that we can determine what a full life consists of and understand the conditions of its realization.

Happiness, according to Aristotelian studies, is not based upon pleasure (though it does not exclude it), nor on richness, power, and glory, but upon a virtuous life (with excellence). Furthermore, a virtuous man would show discernment (guided by wisdom and prudence) to choose good freely. Therefore, a virtuous man would, for Aristotle, be the happiest of men. Friendship, for him, was an implied virtue and, at the same time, was a condition for and symptom of happiness.

In Aristotelian thought, Man's behaviour to their own self, searching a noble demeanour, one based on virtue, results in the behaviour they will demonstrate towards their fellows and, by extension, towards the whole community. In *The Nicomachean Ethics*, Aristotle relates friendship to happiness, and describes it as the exercise of reciprocal benevolence. In other words, according to the Greek philosopher, friendship exists when two people want the good for each other and, therefore, exercise the good mutually. It is possible to find in Tolkien's novel, as well as in its film adaptation,[7] elements that establish a dialogue with the Aristotelian concept of friendship and show how these relationships as represented in the work contribute to the realization of the story, or stories, both in its development and outcome.

---

6. Catunda, R.R.B. Considerações iniciais sobre a eudaimonía e as excelências na *Ética a Nicômaco*. *Polymatheia Revista de Filosofia*, Fortaleza, v.4, n.5, 2008, pp. 127–144.
7. We will be looking at the story from the point of view of the movies too, after all many people know *The Lord of the Rings* only through its cinematographic adaptation, directed by Peter Jackson.

Based upon Aristotle's teleological study, aiming at Man's ends, this book will also be founded upon Christian theology, according to J.R.R. Tolkien's personal beliefs. It is in Thomas Aquinas's *Summa Theologiae*, particularly regarding Charity, that we will find elements that are bound to perfect this discussion. For Aquinas, Charity is a kind of friendship, and his studies take into account the Aristotelian thought, Aristotle being the most cited classical philosopher in the *Summa Theologiae*, which is in turn the most important reference work for theological studies in the Catholic Church and for many protestant theologians.

Just like his friend and Oxford colleague Clive Staples Lewis (1898–1963), author of *The Chronicles of Narnia*, Tolkien was a Christian apologist in a time when followers of Catholicism in England were frequently marginalised. But he vehemently avoided allegorical resources to build his stories, defending "applicability" instead of "allegory".

The author of *The Lord of the Rings* did not include religious thought in the shape of metaphors in his works, but he searched, more than anything, for a story that would please him. This, however, does not exclude the fact that his words are pervaded by the Christian spirit. "Myth and fairy story, he believed, must contain moral and religious truth, but allusively, not explicitly".[8]

Happiness and its synonyms

If you bought this book, you already know how the story ends: Sauron's Ring is finally destroyed, and peace reigns in Middle-earth... until new adventures come about.[9] According

---

8. Duriez, Colin. *Tolkien and C.S. Lewis: the gift of friendship*. New Jersey: Hidden Spring, 2003, p. 41.

9. Those who have read the books, and not only watched the movies, know that Tolkien did not end his saga with the destruction of the Ring: the narrative goes on for about a hundred pages after that, not counting appendices. Besides Aragorn's coronation and Frodo's departure to the Undying Lands, new conflicts arise when the Hobbits return to the Shire, which had been taken by Sharkey, as Saruman had become known there.

to Tolkien's studies, fairy-stories (the genre from which sprang modern fantasy, of which Tolkien's work is part) have among their characteristics the consolation of a happy ending. Tolkien coined a name for that: *eucatastrophe*, a kind of positive catastrophe. Having Aristotle's ethics in mind, which was based on teleology, the study of ends, we will see how the friendship relationships among characters in *The Lord of the Rings*, both in the book and movies, contribute to the established goal in Tolkien's story: the destruction of the Ring.

The eucatastrophic outcome brings about the union of heroes in the story, based upon the friendship kind of love. We will see how these relations contribute to the development of the narrative, because the path the characters tread is also very important in the characters' journey. The virtuous (or vicious) behaviour of each of them interferes in the goal of the story, resulting in the personal, interpersonal, and communal good or evil.

The importance of studying friendship in such a work gains a broad dimension, insofar as friendship is "most necessary to our life" and "not only an indispensable, but also a beautiful or noble thing".[10] It is necessary, therefore, to recognise where such a vital nobility, or its absence, is bestowed (or not) upon the attitudes of primary characters such as Frodo, Gandalf, Gollum, Denethor, Sam, and other ones present in the inspiring saga of *The Lord of the Rings*.

Based upon Aristotle's work, we will analyse friendship in characters both from the literary and the filmic works. The next chapter has two main objectives: to introduce Tolkien's ethical, aesthetic, and religious line of thought, and examine the concepts of friendship provided by Aristotle. It will help us understand better Tolkien's views and show why the choice for *The Nicomachean Ethics* is the most adequate for the present study.

---

10. Aristotle. *The Nicomachean Ethics*, trans. by F. H. Peters, 10 edn. London: Kegan Paul, Trench, Trübner & Co., 1906.

The intention here is not to be excessively theoretical, but to point out aspects which are inherent to human necessity, both from a personal point of view and a political-communal one, considering the theme and object to be discussed. Such as in Tolkien's narrative, in which characters developed personally and collectively, we can also grow as individuals and citizens in our real, Primary World by exercising friendship.

This reflection aims not only to examine how society contributes to the production of works, but also how it receives new ideas and how it can perceive different paths through literature and cinema. We believe that culture is both a means of pleasure and contemplation and an opportunity to reflect upon personal and social values.

Movie language

Given that *The Lord of the Rings* movie trilogy attracts large numbers of spectators — many know the story only because of the movies — it is convenient to say something about the importance of including the cinematographic point of view in the study of friendship relations. Comparative literature scholars defend this methodology as an efficient means to deepen knowledge. Hutcheson Macaulay Posnett[11] affirms that the comparative method is as old as reason, and that imagination, more than experience, works through comparison. We believe that comparison is a basic method to develop any study, since it helps us deepen our knowledge on the object and the theme encountered.

Through comparison, a scientist discovers features that are unique to their object, features that make it what it is and not something else. For instance, one knows what a chair is not only by its function, but through comparison with other objects: it enables one to distinguish it not only from a table,

11. Carvalhal, T. and Coutinho, E. (orgs.). *Literatura Comparada — textos fundadores* [Comparative Literature — founding texts]. Rio de Janeiro: Rocco, 2011.

which has a different function, but also from a bench, which has almost the same function, i.e. to sit. Another example: one knows, for instance, how to distinguish a leopard from a lion judging by their observable similarities and differences. This does not establish, however, a hierarchy of values among the compared objects, but this practice allows us to know them better.

Besides that, knowing the other compared object may lead to broader questions. By analysing the book and the movie based on it, we verify how each artistic expression, written and audiovisual, presents their approach on the theme of friendship, with different elements.

The choice for a comparative method is also related to our view that there is a clear connection between literature and society. It has already been mentioned that many readers, especially young readers, met Tolkien's books through their filmic adaptations. Other people went to the movie theatre because they were already avid readers of Tolkien. Still other people know the story only through the movies and have never read the story. However, the amount of readers who did not allow their personal image of the books to be contaminated by Peter Jackson's movies is not so representative, and even then, they might have had some contact with the movies via banners showing the actors in full costume, for instance.

In other words, nowadays we are immersed in an environment pervaded by visual prompts, and in which cinematographic adaptations are more and more frequent, with movies being released, sometimes, while the literary work is still being written, as evidenced by *Harry Potter*, for instance. Because of that, examining literary and filmic works means adding to the study social factors that interfere in the relation between the public and the work.

According to Vera Follain, the view of the book and the author as superior works and individuals must be changed, because the readers' attitude has changed: they show now a more extensive reading and have become a co-creator of the work. Furthermore, the book ceases to be considered a finished masterpiece and makes room for the "text in continual reworking".[12]

[...] One realizes that, differently from the modern categories, the text is increasingly ceasing to be seen as a work closed in itself, and it is starting to be considered from its connections within a broad network made of numerous other texts, in a decentralized way.[13]

It is necessary to reinforce that we are not trying here to establish a hierarchy of values between book and movie by means of comparison. The intention, rather, is to deepen the knowledge about the theme — friendship — verifying how the same work is articulated across media, going from a printed text into a new platform, involving image, motion, and sound, about half a century after the publication of the literary work.

It is to be highlighted that we agree with the line of thought of scholars such as Ismail Xavier and Robert Stam, who postulate that the notion of fidelity between movie and book is not accepted anymore — up to a sensible extent — because the media are different, independent, and have their own language. We understand, therefore, that both the book and the movie trilogy are a means of communication with their audience, bringing up their own proposals and views of the same story: "instead of a mere 'portrait' of a pre-existing reality, both the novel and the film are communicative expressions, socially located and historically shaped".[14]

Peter Jackson's movies are the first live action productions of *The Lord of the Rings*. In 1977, *The Hobbit* was adapted into an animation for television, produced by Ranking/Bass and 77 minutes long. *The Lord of the Rings* was also adapted into an animation by Ralph Bakshi in 1978, and spectators'

---

12. Follain, V. 'Narrativas em trânsito'. *Revista Contracampo.* Niterói, n.21, 2010, pp. 26-39.
13. Id., p. 28.
14. Stam, R. 'Teoria e prática da adaptação: da fidelidade à intertextualidade'. *Ilha do Desterro*, Florianópolis, n.51, jul./dez. 2006, pp. 19-53.

opinions were divided. For a long time, *The Lord of the Rings* was thought impossible to be transposed into film or any other media that used images as its main sign.

In 2001, the first feature movie of the novel was released, *The Lord of the Rings: The Fellowship of the Ring*, followed by *The Lord of the Rings: The Two Towers* (2002), and *The Lord of the Rings: The Return of the King* (2003), directed and produced by Peter Jackson, and distributed by New Line Cinema. The three movies proved blockbusters, and made almost 3 billion dollars, winning several awards at the Baftas, the Academy Awards and the Golden Globes. *The Return of the King* alone won eleven Oscars and four Golden Globes. In total, the three movies won seventeen Oscar statuettes.

Chapter Two

Ethics and aesthetics in Tolkien's imagination

John Ronald Reuel Tolkien led an ordinary life according to the standards of his time: he held a permanent job position as a professor at Oxford University, he was married to the same woman for more than fifty years and was the devoted father of four children. When one gets to know his biography, one sees that, apart from being a family-oriented man, the Professor was someone of extraordinary inventiveness, intelligence, and acuity; a thinker who knew how to connect the ideas of his time to the wisdom of tradition.

Therefore, analysing friendship in *The Lord of the Rings*, his greatest fictional work, implies knowing a little of his own life and getting closer to his way of thinking, especially to the way he conceived his imagined world — important traits that reverberate in his literary work. Thus, it is essential to study authors who helped build Tolkien's worldview, his relationship with religion, and his ideas about the ethics and aesthetics surrounding literature, mythology, and fairy-stories.

The Professor

John Ronald Reuel Tolkien was born at the end of the nineteenth century, in 1892. From 1916 to 1917 he served in the British Army, during World War I, in the Battle of the Somme. However, due to a fever caused by lice (known as "trench fever"), he returned home earlier than planned. In this battle, he lost two friends who, with him, were part of the TCBS[1]: Robert Quilter Gilson and Geoffrey Bache Smith.

---

1. *Tea Club Barrovian Society*, a school group at King Edward's School, Birmingham, formed in 1910 by Tolkien and three other friends who discussed various matters, including literature.

Some days before his death, Smith wrote to Tolkien, who had already returned to England: "May God bless you my dear John Ronald and may you say things I have tried to say long after I am not there to say them if such be my lot".[2]

Tolkien's friendship with Christopher Wiseman, the fourth member of the TCBS, lasted until the end of his life, and Tolkien had such an admiration for Wiseman that he even named his third son after his friend. In a letter addressed to Wiseman, four months before his death at 81, he says: "Your most devoted friend. Yrs. JRRT. TCBS".[3]

Tolkien's period in the war inspired him to write the beginning of a series of stories that were rewritten several times until they posthumously became what we now know as *The Silmarillion*,[4] a collection of mythological stories created by Tolkien that serve as background for the two main works of fiction he published during his lifetime: *The Hobbit* and *The Lord of the Rings*. The horror of war remained in his mind and helped him describe scenes of battles, death, pain, and anguish.

Friendship was also present in the beginning of the relationship between Tolkien and Edith Bratt, his great love who would later become his wife. They first met each other while lodging at Mrs. Faulkner's house, since they were both orphans. He was sixteen and was accompanied by his brother Hilary, two years younger, and she was nineteen. But they would only start a relationship five years later, since Father Francis Morgan, the boys' guardian, forbade Tolkien to continue meeting Edith until his 21st birthday.

---

2. Duriez, Colin. *Tolkien and C.S. Lewis: the gift of friendship.* New Jersey: Hidden Spring, 2003, p. 16.
3. Tolkien, J.R.R., Carpenter, H. (Org.), Tolkien, C. (Assist.). *The Letters of J.R.R. Tolkien.* London: HarperCollins, 2006, Letter 350, p. 429.
4. Back then, Tolkien gave to these writings the title *The Book of Lost Tales*. They are included in the two initial volumes of the twelve-book series *The History of Middle-earth* (1983-1996). Christopher Tolkien, assisted by the Canadian writer Guy Gavriel Kay, edited a large amount of his father's drafts, and published *The Silmarillion* in 1977.

Tolkien lost his father, Arthur, when he was only four, and his mother when he was twelve. Afterwards, he and his brother were brought up by Father Francis Morgan, a friend of their mother's, Mabel Tolkien.

After becoming a widow, Mabel converted to Catholicism, in 1900, along with her sister May, and because of that she suffered rejection from her Methodist family. Tolkien's biographer, Humphrey Carpenter, says that May was forbidden by her husband, Walter Incledon, to convert to Catholicism, but Mabel stood firm in her decision.

Her brother-in-law had helped Mabel financially since Arthur's death but, after her conversion to the Catholic Church, he ceased to assist her and her children. Financial difficulties, along with the rejection by her family and the Tolkiens — mostly Baptists — led to Mabel's poor health, and she died of diabetes four years after her conversion.

Two years after joining the Catholic Church, Mabel met Father Francis Xavier Morgan who, apart from being her confessor, was a friend of the family and, later, Ronald[5] and Hilary's guardian when they became orphans. Father Morgan was like a second father for the boys, and this provided Tolkien with a better integration to Christian faith. Ronald, who was to become a famous writer of fantasy, had, therefore, strong links to Catholicism, which led him to a profound knowledge of faith.

His religious conviction was so strong that it significantly contributed to C.S. Lewis's conversion to Christianity.[6] They both worked at Oxford and were part of the literary group *The Inklings*.[7] They would also have important dialogues about

---

5. J.R.R. Tolkien's second name, by which his family addressed him.

6. Lewis was born into a protestant family but declared himself atheist at the age of fifteen. In 1929, he converted to Christianism and eventually joined the Anglican church.

7. The Inklings were an informal literary group in Oxford. Besides Tolkien and Lewis, the latter being the core of the group, it had eleven other regular members, among them the poet Charles Williams and Tolkien's son, Christopher. There were also occasional attendants, such as Owen Barfield.

their respective writings, particularly *The Lord of the Rings*, which Lewis received with encouragement and enthusiasm.

Tolkien was a philologist and professor of Old English at the University of Oxford and, apart from the bureaucratic issues of his office, he took much pleasure in his work. He was passionate about words and about several languages, particularly Finnish and Welsh, which inspired the phonology of his fictitious languages spoken by the Elves: Quenya and Sindarin. In a letter to his North American publishing house, Houghton Mifflin Co., Tolkien wrote: "To me a name comes first and the story follows".[8]

Tolkien and Lewis's friendship was based on shared preferences, but also many differences, especially before Lewis's conversion. According to *The Gift of Friendship*, which deals with the friendly relationship between both fantasy authors, in the beginning Lewis, author of *The Chronicles of Narnia*, declared himself a naturalist: he thought that "every finite thing or event must be (in principle) explicable in terms of the Total System".[9] Tolkien, in turn, had always been a supernaturalist. In his essay *On Fairy-stories*, included in the book *Tree and Leaf*, he wrote: "Nature is no doubt a life-study, […] but there is a part of man which is not 'Nature', and which therefore is not obliged to study it, and is, in fact, wholly unsatisfied by it".[10]

Shortly before Lewis's conversion, the ideas they both had about imagination started to converge, especially regarding studies of language and literature. They thought that these should turn to the Middle Ages and Classical Antiquity, putting aside romanticism, the then prevailing view at Oxford. Duriez points out a comment by Lewis that summarises the Tolkien-Lewis attitude: "If you take your stand on the 'prevalent' view, how long do you suppose it will prevail? […] All you can really

8. Tolkien, J.R.R., Carpenter, H. (Org.), Tolkien, C. (Assist.). *The Letters of J.R.R. Tolkien*. Op. cit., Letter 165, p. 219.
9. Lewis, quoted in Duriez, *Tolkien and C.S. Lewis*. Op. cit., p. 27.
10. Tolkien, J.R.R. 'On Fairy-stories', in *Tree and Leaf*. London: HarperCollins, 2001, p. 77.

say about my taste is that it is old-fashioned; yours will soon be the same".[11]

Tolkien's (and Lewis's) philosophical basis was grounded, thus, on the medieval and classical thought, and not on the rationalist one; nor did they anchor their criticism about modernity on romanticism. Such medieval and classical lines were in harmony with Tolkien's personal taste, and were the source of his research and work, as evidenced by the medieval epic poem *Beowulf* (copied in the 11th century), which he translated from Old to Modern English in 1926, without ever finishing editing it.[12] Another work of reference translated by Tolkien was *Sir Gawain and the Green Knight*, a romance from the 14th century based on the legend of King Arthur and the Knights of the Round Table.

Subcreative fantasy

The Silmarillion contains five stories, among which the *Quenta Silmarillion* is the main one. It starts with the *Ainulindalë*, which means "The Music of the Ainur" in Quenya, the elvish language invented by Tolkien. In this account, Eru Ilúvatar, the Creator of everything that exists in Tolkien's fictional world, introduces a theme to the Ainur,[13] and they develop this theme in musical form, struggling, each group in their own fashion, to comprehend part of Ilúvatar's thought, seeking harmony in their composition. By listening to the others, they managed to shape a single composition, beautiful and harmonic.

Melkor, the most powerful among the Ainur, decided to put into the Music parts that he invented himself, which were not originally present in Eru's mind, thus generating disarrangement and disharmony. At first Eru, with a smile, raises his left hand, proposing a new theme. Once again Melkor starts a dissonance, to which Eru, now stern, raises his

---

11. Lewis quoted in Duriez, *Tolkien and C.S. Lewis. Op. cit.*, pp. 26-27.
12. In 2014, Tolkien's translation of *Beowulf* was launched by HarperCollins.
13. Immortal spirits similar to the angels in the Christian doctrine.

right hand, demanding a third song to be made. But Melkor resumes his disarrangement and then Eru, with a face "terrible to behold", raising both hands, puts an end to the symphony of the Ainur. The last theme originates the universe, called Eä, which transforms the ideas of the Ainur, based on Eru's thoughts, into the physical world.

The creation of the world includes also the existence of the Children of Ilúvatar —Elves and Men — who were not present in the imagination of the Ainur, but solely in Eru's, the One. Among the Ainur who entered the physical world, the most powerful ones were called Valar, and the ones with lesser power, Maiar.[14]

Tolkien's creativity does not end there. A sizeable proportion of his *legendarium* — the term used by the author himself, comprising the whole mythology he invented — was handed over to us, metalinguistically, by means of a fictional story written on the *Red Book of Westmarch*, mainly authored by the Hobbits Bilbo, Frodo, Sam, and his descendants. The stories in there deal especially with the adventures told in *The Hobbit* and *The Lord of the Rings*.

This brief description was meant to show a fragment of the dimension of Tolkien's work and mind. We also know that the author's view of imagination, and his religious and moral conceptions, contributed significantly to the fictional, aesthetic and, most of all, ethical output of *The Lord of the Rings*. However, it is necessary to stress that Tolkien, as opposed to what he saw in his friend C.S. Lewis's works, rejected the notion of allegory in his fiction. For him, the more applicability a work of literature contained, the richer it would be. In the preface to *The Lord of the Rings*, he explains:

> [...] I cordially dislike allegory in all its manifestations, and always have done so [...] I much prefer history, true or feigned, with its varied applicability to the thought and experience of readers. I

---

14. The singular words are, respectively, Vala and Maia. The feminine of Vala is Valië (plural Valier).

think that many confuse 'applicability' with 'allegory'; but the one resides in the freedom of the reader, and the other in the purposed domination of the author.[15]

It is clear that, even though the Christian spirit pervaded *The Lord of the Rings*, as we shall see further on, it is not supposed to be a religious work, despite the presence of the author's religious morality in his works and in his approach to Myth. Valter Henrique Fritsch claims that works such as *The Lord of the Rings*, by Tolkien, *The Chronicles of Narnia*, by Lewis, *The Neverending Story*, by Michael Ende, and other stories constitute the genre called Fantasy, and share traces of the Myth combined with characteristics of Marvellous tales.

Quoting Joseph Campbell, Fritsch states that such works approach the Myth by bringing a series of symbols "that help the human individual understand the world surrounding them and take them through a journey of evolution".[16] We know that the Myth has always had a religious function, remarkably oral in its attempt to explain the ritual. However, with the advent of literature, Myth gave way to the laicization of Word, and literature started to include the myths in its stories, similarly to other artistic manifestations, like music, cinema, and other visual and plastic arts.

Fritsch recalls statements by the mythologists Joseph Campbell and Mircea Eliade, who claim that "the myths reveal the inner work of human psyche".[17] The Brazilian Tolkienist Ronald Kyrsme adds: "The quality of the myth, for Tolkien, is that it conveys fundamental and timeless truths in an easily assimilable way".[18] That is why even the staunchest atheists can be enchanted by a Tolkien's work: when they enter the mythological world, his writings touch what a human being

15. Tolkien, J.R.R. *The Lord of the Rings*. London: HarperCollins, 2008, p. xxviii.
16. Fritsch, V.H. 'Atravessando Limiares: Simbologias de Passagem no Romance de Fantasia'. *Recorte*. Três Corações, n.1, v.11, p. 1-14, jan.-jun. 2014, p. 2.
17. Ibid.
18. Kyrmse, R. *Explicando Tolkien*. São Paulo: Martins Fontes, 2003, p. 23.

has in their deepest and most intimate part, without being connected to the religious discourse.

In his book *The Hero with a Thousand Faces*, Joseph Campbell makes an account of several myths in world culture and comes up with the thesis of the monomyth: all myths tell the same story in varied versions. Thus, every mythological hero undertakes a more or less similar journey.

Some of the milestones in a hero's adventure are the call to leave behind their ordinary life, the refusal followed by acceptance of the mission, the contact with a mentor or supernatural aid, the trials phase, the contact with the world of shadows or of death, the supreme ordeal, the accomplishment of the objective, the reward, the return, and the bringing of the elixir which will benefit all the hero's friends.

Tolkien's concept of the myth approaches and simultaneously deviates from Campbell's. One of the thinkers who inspired Tolkien the most in several subjects, including fantasy and myth, was the philosopher, journalist, and writer Gilbert Keith Chesterton. He said it would be a great mistake to deal with myth and folklore in a rationalist fashion, given that they are "a work of imagination and, therefore, a work of art".[19] For him, mythic and folkloric stories should only be analysed from an inside point of view, not from the outside as though they were scientific objects.

According to Chesterton, the artists, consciously or not, sought to awaken hidden realities in a spiritual plane, by means of imagination and beauty.[20] However, he rejects the attribution of religious status to myth in the same way it is attributed to Christianism, because the latter is, for him, a combination of imagination and reason (and faith, one might add), whereas the myth lives only in the plane of imagination. He affirms:

---

19. Chesterton, G.K. *The Everlasting Man.* London: Hodder & Stoughton Ltd., 1928, p. 116.
20. Id., pp. 120-121.

> [...] the Church was actually the first thing that ever tried to combine reason and religion. There had never before been any such union of the priests and the philosophers. Mythology, then, sought God through the imagination; or sought truth by means of beauty [...][21]

In 1931, Tolkien, Lewis, and Hugo Dyson — another Oxford scholar and member of The Inklings — had a discussion about myth which makes Tolkien's view on the matter quite explicit. Back then, he and Dyson were Catholic, while Lewis, in the process of conversion, was a theist, but not a Christian apologist as he would come to be. Tolkien and Dyson defended that myths, in their own way, carried part of the Divine Truth revelation, while Lewis insisted on the view that they were nothing but lies, even though he had a personal interest in Norse mythologies.

Reinaldo José Lopes, in his dissertation *A Árvore de Estórias: uma proposta de tradução para* Tree and Leaf, *de J.R.R. Tolkien,* offers a translation, into Portuguese, for Tolkien's poem "Mythopoeia". Put simply, it is the poetic incarnation of Tolkien's discussion with Lewis. Lopes says:

> Such a perspective, in great measure awaken by Tolkien's profound catholic faith, regards the "making of myths" ([...] *Mythopoeia*) as the most authentic human activity, as opposed to the vain efforts (if not totally perverse) to enslave nature by means of technology. [...] According to the biographer [Humphrey Carpenter], the dedication of the poem (which compares myths to "lies breathed through silver") was originally said by Lewis himself. Similarly, Philomythus (the myth-lover) is Tolkien, while Misomythos (the myth-hater) represents Lewis.[22]

Lopes emphasises that Tolkien was not, strictly speaking, against technology and science – after all, his own profession depended on the exercise of reason – but "he feared the dehumanising effects of a worldview which tries to restrict

---

21. Chesterton, G.K. *The Everlasting Man.* Op. cit., p. 128.
22. Lopes, R.J. *A Árvore de Estórias: uma proposta de tradução para* Tree and Leaf, *de J.R.R. Tolkien.* 2006. Master's thesis, pp. 148-149.

reality solely to what is perceptible and measurable, or which eliminates the spiritual dimension".[23]

Later, completely converted, Lewis developed what Tolkien already defended: that myths, in a way or another, reflect (part of) the truth of the great Christian myth, which is also a myth inasmuch as it crosses human imagination. In his book *God in the Dock*, Lewis published the text "Myth Became Fact", in which he writes:

> Now as myth transcends thought, incarnation transcends myth. The heart of Christianity is a myth which is also a fact. The old myth of the dying god, without ceasing to be myth, comes down from the heaven of legend and imagination to the earth of history.
> [...]
> We pass from a Balder or an Osiris, dying nobody knows when or where, to a historical person crucified (it is all in order) under Pontius Pilate. By becoming fact it does not cease to be myth: that is the miracle.[24]

Mythopoeia, then, becomes an important feature in some fantastic novels, especially *The Lord of the Rings*, and in other artistic manifestations of similar genre: to bring a mythical universe in a fictional level (literature and other aesthetic categories), created by a single author/artist or a group of authors/artists, with the maximum amount of detail concerning the invented world, making it more acceptable to their public. It is possible to say that Tolkien is the icon of this ability in contemporaneity, given his ambitious project of building a mythology in English.

This quality, which conveys the text as convincingly as possible to the reader, is called verisimilitude, and comprises the "inner consistency of reality", mentioned by Tolkien in his essay *On Fairy-stories*. The better a work of fantasy is elaborated, the more real it becomes to the reader.

---

23. Id., p. 149.
24. Lewis, C.S. *God in the Dock*. Michigan/Cambridge: Wm B. Eerdmans Publishing Co., 2014, pp. 58-59.

Ronald Kyrmse, in his *Explicando Tolkien*, emphasises an important aspect of the author's inventive capacity: the *tri-dimensionality of his work*. This means that Tolkien's work has basically three dimensions: *diversity*, *depth*, and *time*. The first one has to do with the vastness of his created world, including specificities of botany, linguistics, geography etc. *Depth* has to do with the fact that each mode of knowledge in there is rich in detail: one can, for instance, find in Tolkien's stories not only different words spoken by the Elves, but created languages which are full of semantic, syntactical, morphological, and etymological details. The third dimension, *time*, relates to the three Ages Tolkien created: his subcreated world, diverse and deep, is subjected to changes from the creation of the universe to the Fourth Age, Men's Age, which is the beginning of what we understand today, our History.

A mythopoeic work, such as Tolkien's, is not associated to oral tradition such as myths, and does not set itself to explain religious rituals, nor is it the product of many centuries. It takes shape in the mind of its creator, or *subcreator*, as the Professor suggests.

Tolkien coined the word "subcreation" in his *On Fairy-stories*. This concept departs from the principle that every existing thing is part of divine creation.[25] Our creativity, therefore, would for Tolkien come from our ability to perceive the elements of creation, particularly the qualities of each existing thing. By comprehending them we would be able to open the doors to other possibilities. We would be able, thus, to *subcreate*. "Fantasy remains a human right: we make in our measure and in our derivative mode, because we are made: and not only made, but made in the image and likeness of a Maker".[26]

Tolkien calls the world of concrete reality and everything that is possible *Primary World*, and the reality that is subcreated by our mind, as well as every desirable thing, he calls *Secondary*

---

25. The theory of how the world would have been created – from the point of view of Creationism or Evolutionism – is not at stake here.
26. Tolkien, J.R.R. *Tree and Leaf*. Op. cit., p. 56.

World. Thus, it does not do to ask if fantasy is true or not, because the Primary World establishes what is *possible* and the Secondary World that which is *desirable*. As "art", however, within the invented world it must be true to exist, otherwise the subcreator will have failed.

Tolkien defended fantasy as something natural for the human being, just like reason seeks scientific truth. Reason itself would be in the service of fantasy, because the more one knows the created Primary World, the richer the subcreated Secondary World.

> The human mind, endowed with the powers of generalization and abstractions, sees not only *green-grass*, discriminating it from other things […], but sees that it is green as well as being grass. But how powerful, how stimulating to the very faculty that produced it, was the invention of the adjective: no spell or incantation in Faërie is more potent.[27]

The work of the subcreative artist requires that the maximum amount of detail be added to that invented reality. This conception about how fantastic art works upon the fairy-stories greatly reflects the way Tolkien wrote his stories. His short story "Leaf by Niggle" (part of the book *Tree and Leaf*) is considered by some his most allegorical writing inasmuch as it may be seen as a self-description, more clearly seen when one analyses the way Tolkien and the protagonist work. Niggle, the central character, is a punctilious painter who spends his days painting a canvas, but he never finishes it: he wants to paint a tree but pauses carefully on each leaf. *The Lord of the Rings*, in turn, is the result of a whole life of research by Tolkien, of tireless and meticulous labour, resulting in a plot pervaded by adventure, languages, poems, calendars, maps, and what not.

Tolkien, when talking about fairy-stories, claimed that the magic of these narratives consists of awakening the primary

---

27. Id., p. 22, emphasis by the author.

human desires: to inspect the depths of space and time and to be in communion with other living beings. Fairy-stories, for Tolkien, are worthy reading for adults as well as any other literary genre. They have their artistic value and, besides, they offer "*Fantasy, Recovery, Escape* and *Consolation,* all things of which children have, as a rule, less need than older people".[28]

With the word *fantasy* Tolkien refers precisely to the access to the world of imagination, the supernatural, the magical, the mythic, the Secondary World which does not exist in fact but in our desire. It contains the product of subcreation, brought about by the artistic operation of our imagination, plus a "captivating strangeness", the extraordinary, that thing which, by means of attributing adjectives to what already exists, becomes something we do not see in our Primary World.

As for *recovery,* the fairy-stories purportedly have the mission of restoring the human perception of reality, helping them to see the world again as novel after gaining in fantasy some sort of "ammunition". "I do not say 'seeing things as they are', […] though I might venture to say 'seeing things as we are (or were) meant to see them' — as things apart from ourselves".[29]

Fairy-stories also offer to the reader escape, which is often misunderstood. Tolkien warns: "they are confusing, not always by sincere error, the Escape of the Prisoner with the Flight of the Deserter".[30] The Secondary World stories bring the necessary freedom from the everyday vices that imprison us. With that, Tolkien criticises the ephemerality of modernity, scientism, and exacerbated rationalism. Escape, in this case, prioritises what is long-lasting, such as nature. "Fairy-stories may invent monsters that fly the air or dwell in the deep, but at least they do not try to escape from heaven or the sea".[31]

---

28. Tolkien, J.R.R. *Tree and Leaf.* Op. cit., p. 46.
29. Id., pp. 57-58.
30. Id., p. 61.
31. Id., p. 63.

Consolation and happiness

Fairy-stories also present as a main characteristic the *consolation*, which is built upon our deepest desire for escape: death. The stories from the Enchanted Realm bring the comfort of a happy ending, not in a naïve and childish way, but with the conviction that such happiness is the fate of human nature, as long as one uses well one's freedom. To describe that, Tolkien coins a new term: *eucatastrophe*.

> [...] Tragedy is the true form of Drama, its highest function; but the opposite is true of Fairy-story. Since we do not appear to possess a word that expresses this opposite — I will call it *Eucatastrophe*. The *eucatastrophic* tale is the true form of fairy-tale, and its highest function.[32]

The *eucatastrophe*, which translates as "good catastrophe", has a religious background, based on the Christian gospels. The happy ending of fairy-stories, with a sudden, victorious turn, mirrors Christ's life, who, according to the gospels, passed from death in the sepulchre into resurrection and redemption. Tolkien argues that this joy

> is not essentially 'escapist', nor 'fugitive'. In its fairy-tale – or otherworld – setting, it is a sudden and miraculous grace: never to be counted on to recur. It does not deny the existence of *dyscatastrophe*, of sorrow and failure: the possibility of these is necessary to the joy of deliverance; it denies [...] universal final defeat and in so far is *evangelium*, giving a fleeting glimpse of Joy [...].[33]

The eucatastrophic ending engages in a dialogue with the ultimate end of the supreme good, which Aristotle proposes in *The Nicomachean Ethics*. The philosopher says:

> If then in what we do there be some end which we wish for on its own account, choosing all the others as means to this, but not every

32. Id., p. 68.
33. Id., p. 69.

end without exception as a means to something else (for so we should go on *ad infinitum*, and desire would be left void and objectless), — this evidently will be the good or the best of all things.[34]

The supreme good is what we understand, in our culture, as happiness. One does not wish to be happy in order to achieve something. On the contrary, we want to achieve some things in order to be happy. Aristotle clarifies this by saying that happiness is absolute, self-sufficing, the end of an action:

> And further, happiness is believed to be the most desirable thing in the world, and that not merely as one among other good things: if it were merely one among other good things [...], it is plain that the addition of the least of other goods must make it more desirable; for the addition becomes a surplus of good, and of two goods the greater is always more desirable.
>
> Thus it seems that happiness is something final and self-sufficing, and is the end of all that man does.[35]

If we pore over the proposed resolution for the problem we set in this work, peace in Middle-earth achieved by the destruction of the Ring, we will see that the ultimate end of the saga is what affords its happy conclusion. However, we know that dyscatastrophe, that is, the possibility of sorrow and failure, is not denied, and still is a condition for the triumph of good: before defeating Sauron, Frodo and his fellows experience many battles and ordeals. The presence of true friends is evidently essential for the concretization of the eucatastrophe, the desired happiness in the face of challenge.

One must bear in mind also that the story does not end after the Ring is destroyed. The book brings further smaller adventures and new minor, yet troublesome, obstacles such as the wizard Saruman afflicting the Shire. This demonstrates Tolkien's conviction that, in life, complete happiness cannot be achieved. In this postmodern story, apart from the multiplicity

---

34. Aristotle. *The Nicomachean Ethics*, trans. by F. H. Peters, 10 edn. London: Kegan Paul, Trench, Trübner & Co., 1906, p. 2.
35. Id., pp. 14-15.

of (defectible) heroes, the happy ending is not definitive, or at least it is not so in the material world — even though it leaves room for faith in a supernatural world, where such completeness is achieved.

As it has been made clear, however, this analysis focuses on the main objective of the story: the destruction of the One Ring to bring back peace among the free peoples of Middle-earth. This is our happy ending, the final good of this narrative "frame". Peter Jackson's filmic adaption was also based on it: the movies did not include the chapter "The Scouring of the Shire", although some references to it were included in the *The Return of the King*.

The ending that denies defeatism in the world is centred on the portrayal of heroes who, despite their failures, are worthy of eucatastrophe. Vladimir Propp, in his *Morphology of the Folktale*, presents two kinds of hero: the one who suffers the consequences of an antagonist and the one who repairs misfortunes or sees to the necessity of others. In Tolkien's saga, the central characters fit better the second category of heroes, especially when one thinks about Frodo.

The strongest ones in Tolkien's story are precisely the humblest: Frodo is only a Hobbit, the most forgotten people in Middle-earth. The good nature of virtuous individuals is, thus, essential for the portrayal of the hero, because they bring good in themselves and wish well to others who, if they are like-natured, will return such benevolence reciprocally. And such is what happens with friendship also.

Because of friendship, or of principles that might lead to it, the image of the hero, as said before, can be present not only in a single character, but in many. Frodo alone would not be able to reach Mordor to destroy the Ring: he needed the help of Sam, Gandalf, Aragorn, Legolas, Merry, Pippin, Gimli, Galadriel, Éowyn, and many others.

The characters in *The Lord of the Rings* do not always behave in a regular or expected manner within that universe. They waver; they are often hesitant and evolve throughout the story. Boromir, who initially formed *The Fellowship of the Ring*, is to be highlighted: he had the mission of helping Frodo destroy the magical object, but he ends up betraying his friends by trying to take the Ring. Later, when Frodo has already escaped, without telling anyone about his betrayal, Boromir has a redemptive ending: he dies trying to save his friends Merry and Pippin from the claws of the Orcs. Afterwards, both Hobbits will be essential for Sauron's defeat brought about with the destruction of the Ring.

Joseph Campbell describes the hero of fairy-stories as particular, microscopic, and the hero of the myth as universal, macroscopic. In Tolkien's fantasy, both types can be observed: the hero as individual and the hero as archetype. Our theoretical basis about friendship takes the individual character into account, as well as the attitudes that lead to the concretization of this kind of love, resulting, thus, in a communal reality.

The Fantasy genre — joining aspects of myth and marvellous tale — describes Tolkien's works. Using the contribution that fairy-stories provide — fantasy, recovery, escape, and consolation — Tolkien builds his fictional universe, with its heroes and villains that engage in intimate and collective relationship.

Such heroes, in the light of Aristotle's virtue ethics, contribute to the eucatastrophic outcome by exercising friendship, having the idea of happiness as the end which does not desire additional goods. In other words: the presence of friends is essential for the happy ending, and, in opposition, one might say that enmity is the main responsible for the defeat of Evil, because it destroys itself.

Goodness, reciprocity, and communication

In *The Nicomachean Ethics*, Aristotle claims that there are three kinds of friendship,[36] and these are, in turn, divided in

---

36. Aristotle, *Nicomachean Ethics*. Op. cit., p. 255.

two categories, the *accidental* — based on *profit* and *pleasure* — and the *perfect*, based on *mutual well-wishing*.

> Those, therefore, whose love for one another is based on the useful, do not love each other for what they are, but only in so far as each gets some good from the other.
>
> It is the same also with those whose affection is based on pleasure; people care for a wit, for instance, not for what he is, but as the source of pleasure to themselves. [...]
>
> These friendships, then, are "accidental"; for the object of affection is love, not as being the person or character that he is, but as the source of some good or some pleasure. [...]
>
> But the perfect kind of friendship is that of good men who resemble one another in virtue. For they both alike wish well to one another as good men, and it is their essential character to be good men.[37]

According to the philosopher, the perfect friendship lasts long because it is founded upon goodness, which is a long-lasting characteristic. Good people live in virtue, and they are essentially good; and by seeing in a friend another "self", they would be equally good in their relationships.

The (post)modern contrast

For Aristotle, having all these qualities, one would naturally expect friendship to be something rare and that it requires familiarity.[38] It is precisely on this point that we think important to show that Aristotle's definition of friendship may differ from that of modern or contemporary thinkers.[39]

One who directly undertakes this critical evaluation, sharing Tolkien's values, is his friend C.S. Lewis. According

---

37. Id., pp. 255-257.

38. Id., p. 257.

39. Some ideas based on modern rationalism or romantic modernism are very much different from the classical and medieval mode of thinking which were the foundation of Tolkien's own thoughts. However, his line was not a mere copy of old ideas, because he lived in a contemporary context. His ideas, therefore, present new and traditional concepts for the contemporary reader.

to the author of *The Chronicles of Narnia*, friendship has currently become something marginal since few people value or experience it. In his book *The Four Loves*, he claims that friendship is one of the four expressions of love (apart from affection, Eros, and charity), and is the least bound by natural human needs, especially in comparison to Eros (necessary for begetting) and affection (necessary for rearing). Says Lewis:

> This (so to call it) "non-natural" quality in Friendship goes far to explain why it was exalted in ancient and medieval times and has come to be made light of in our own. [...]
> But then came Romanticism and "tearful comedy" and the "return to nature" and the exaltation of Sentiment; and in their train all that great wallow of emotion which, though often criticized, has lasted ever since. Finally, the exaltation of instinct, the dark gods in the blood; whose hierophants may be incapable of male friendship [...]
> Again, that outlook which values the collective above the individual necessarily disparages Friendship; it is a relation between men at their highest level of individuality.[40]

Let us take as an example Hannah Arendt's speech "On Humanity in Dark Times: Thoughts about Lessing", published in the book *Men in Dark Times*, which confirms Lewis's argument. She affirms that the representative of the Enlightenment, Gotthold Ephraim Lessing, saw friendship in a political light, different from the notion of *fraternité* by Jean-Jacques Rousseau and, therefore, different from the fundamental thought of the eighteenth-century French Revolution. Her criticism lay precisely on the concept of fraternity (and, therefore, intimacy), since this had its natural place "among the repressed and persecuted, the exploited and humiliated",[41] and was directly linked to the idea of compassion, through which "the revolutionary-minded humanitarian of the eighteenth century sought to achieve solidarity with the unfortunate and

---

40. Lewis, C.S. *The Four Loves*. New York: Harcourt, Brace, 1960, pp. 89-90.
41. Arendt, H. 'On Humanity in Dark Times: Thoughts about Lessing', translated by Clara and Richard Winston, in Arendt, Hannah, *Men in Dark Times*. New York: Harcourt, Brace, p. 14.

the miserable — an effort tantamount to penetrating the very domain of brotherhood".[42]

Such a phenomenon, according to Arendt, caused great damage to the modern revolutions, benefiting the miserable in a momentary way, but not the collective justice. In a criticism of modernity, Arendt searches the Antiquity for endorsement for the argumentation anchored in Lessing: "Because they so clearly recognized the affective nature of compassion, which can overcome us like fear without our being able to fend it off, the ancients regarded the most compassionate person as no more entitled to be called the best than the most fearful".[43] The author concludes, thus, that the humanitarianism of fraternity could only be concerned with those not wronged by the device of compassion.

For Arendt, compassion, and by extension friendship based on intimacy, had no practical use in political terms, political being understood as collectivity-oriented. She says:

> We are wont to see friendship solely as a phenomenon of intimacy, in which friends open their hearts to each other unmolested by the world and its demands. [...] Thus it is hard for us to understand the political relevance of friendship.[44]

According to her understanding of the ancient Greeks, questionably, as we have demonstrated, friendship was political (from a collective point of view) and not intimate, and it was based essentially upon speech: "For the world is not humane just because it is made by human beings, and it does not become humane just because the human voice sounds in it, but only when it has become the object of discourse".[45]

In this regard, her view conforms to Lessing's thought. He claimed that, between *aletheia* and *doxa* (the truth and the opinion, respectively), a thinker of the Age of Enlightenment would choose the second since, for them, if truth did exist,

---

42. Id., p. 14.
43. Id., p. 15.
44. Id., p. 24.
45. Ibid.

"that would mean an end to discourse and thus to friendship and thus to humanness".[46]

Friendship for Lessing, according to Arendt, was based on the search for a common good, though allowing for divergences, without reference to family proximity or predilection. Otherwise, the intimate friend would invariably become a sibling, and this implies exclusivity, which disagrees with friendship according to this view. She aimed at tolerance and diversity in collectivity, because if truth was established, it could only spring from a single opinion. "Should that happen, the world, which can form only in the interspaces between men in all their variety, would vanish altogether".[47]

According to Arendt's and other postmodern authors' ideas, the classical conception of friendship, linked to compassion, intimacy, and familiarity, was out of place. Opposing to Aristotle's view on friendship — and, consequently, Tolkien's — which regards the fellow human as another self, the postmodern suggestion values sociability, tolerance, and collectivity. The consensus, that is, sharing the same truth, would not be a desired good, and the political thought would prevail with plurality and constant change.

Necessity and the symptom of virtue

The ethics sought for in *The Nicomachean Ethics* is mainly a political one:

> Since then [Politics] makes use of the other practical sciences, and since it further ordains what men are to do and from what to refrain, its end must include the ends of the others, and must be the proper good of man. For though this good is the same for the individual and the state, yet the good of the state seems a grander and more perfect thing both to attain and to secure; and glad as one would be to do this service for a single individual, *to do it for a people and for a number of states is nobler and more divine.*[48]

---

46. Arendt, H. *Men in Dark Times*. Op. cit., p. 26.
47. Id., p. 31.
48. Id., p. 3 (emphasis added).

However, contrary to postmodern discourses, Aristotle claims that perfect friendship requires intimacy, and we know that by means of it one reaches politics, in a collective sphere, since sociability and good disposition are its causes. In the Aristotelian conception, perfect friendship depends on the integrity of character and mutual well-wishing. Friendship (*philia*) is, thus, based upon equality: "Friendly relations to others, and all the characteristics by which friendship is defined, seem to be derived from our relations towards ourselves".[49]

The shaping of friendship, under this perspective, starts from the inner relationship of man with their own self, who then connects with another man, eventually generating a friendly relationship within a whole community, aiming at reaching, by means of virtue, happiness. To explain how that works, we must first examine the association Aristotle made between virtue and the concept of happiness.

First, he dismantles the views that associate happiness with fame, power, richness, or pleasure (even though he does not categorically deny the role of the latter two in some measure). For him, happiness is "an exercise of the vital faculties in accordance with perfect virtue or excellence",[50] because only this exercise in accordance with virtue can bestow stability and durability for the soul, necessary for the highest good (*eudaimonia*), that good which does not desire other goods.

As for virtue, the philosopher describes it as a good based upon the golden mean, the happy medium, which the individual should incorporate as a habit. He says that there are "three classes of disposition, viz. two kinds of vice, one marked by excess, the other by deficiency, and one kind of virtue, the observance of the mean".[51]

This middle ground requires, too, a great deal of common sense: "So much then is plain, that the middle character is in

49. Id., p. 294.
50. Id., p. 30.
51. Id., p. 52.

all cases to be praised, but that we ought to incline sometimes towards excess, sometimes towards deficiency; for in this way shall we most easily hit the mean and attain to right doing."[52]

Besides that, as we have said before, virtue is coupled up with habit, which requires a lifelong behaviour, "for one swallow or one fine day does not make a spring, nor does one day or any small space of time make a blessed or happy man".[53]

"One swallow does not make a spring" has to do not only with time and constancy, but also with the fact that one does not achieve anything on one's own. This means that friendship is not limited to the individual or to the community, but to this movement from inside out: the self, the other, the community. Still in the Aristotelian conception, it is possible to say that a good ruler is one that is inherently good, who practices benevolence towards their intimate ones, and who seeks the well-being of their people.

Lewis was more radical and, maybe to reinforce his antipathy towards the modern/romantic/contemporary thinking, he emphasises friendship as a selective relationship, for him, "when your friend has become an old friend, all those things about him which had originally nothing to do with the friendship become familiar and dear with familiarity".[54]

In Aristotle, friendship depend on loving rather than on being loved, since "the virtue of a friend is to love, so that when people love each other in proportion to their worth, they are lasting friends, and theirs is a lasting friendship".[55] By virtue, the friendship between unequal people would be possible, and it would make them equal:

> This is also the way in which persons who are unequal can be most truly friends; for thus they will make themselves equal: but equality and similarity tend to friendship, and most of all the similarity of

52. Arendt, H. *Men in Dark Times*. Op. cit., p. 57.
53. Id., p. 17.
54. Lewis, C.S. *The Four Loves*. Op. cit., p. 57.
55. Aristotle, *Nicomachean Ethics*. Op. cit., p. 268.

those who resemble each other *in virtue*; for such men, being little liable to change, continue as they were in themselves and to one another, and do not ask anything unworthy of one another, or do anything unworthy for one another — nay, rather restrain one another from anything of the sort; for it is characteristic of a good man neither to go wrong himself, nor to let his friend go wrong.[56]

Regarding politics, Aristotle sets dialogue and opinion as the protagonists of the equation. "Unanimity, then, seems to be, as it is called, the kind of friendship that prevails in states".[57] However, such "conformity" of opinions is not the same as "identity" of opinions: allowing for individual specificities, one says that "unanimity prevails in a state when the citizens agree in their judgments about what is for the common interest, and choose the same course, and carry out the decision of the community".[58] Still, for the philosopher, unanimity, like perfect friendship, is only possible between good people, because they "wish what is just and for the common interest".[59] Thus, they do not make use of word simply to persuade, but aiming at the communal good.

Talking about the kind of love called friendship, C.S. Lewis says that friends are the ones who see the same truth, which presupposes intimacy and exclusiveness. From a political point of view, Lewis goes beyond: groups of friends are like a resistance to power. If we take *The Fellowship of the Ring* as an example, we can see that its members found in their union the strength they needed to fight Sauron. In favour of a common ideal, even with past disagreement between their peoples, such as is the case between the dwarf Gimli and the elf Legolas; they unite and become resistant and, therefore, victorious.

By affirming that friendship springs from a single, shared truth, Lewis criticises the kind of friendship whose objective is only communal, with no bonds:

56. Id., p. 268 (emphasis added).
57. Id., p. 300.
58. Id., p. 299.
59. Id., p. 300.

Hence if our masters [...] ever succeed in producing a world where all are Companions and none are Friends, they will have removed certain dangers, and will also have taken from us what is almost our strongest safeguard against complete servitude.[60]

Friendship in charity

As a theologian, Lewis uses Christianity as a complement to his study about friendship. He devises a beautiful image in which God is responsible for true Friendship, which would, in turn, awaken the Beauty (whose source is the very divine being) of others before us. The Creator chose our friends before we did, and He chose to be everyone's Friend.

In Tolkien's mythology, as previously seen, there is Eru Ilúvatar, a fictional character that plays the role of the Jewish Christian God, the creator of that fantastic world, even though He is not explicitly mentioned in *The Lord of the Rings*.[61] Tolkien, although he rejected allegorical interpretations, did not accept the claim that religion was not present in his works. He wrote about it in one of his letters: "It is a monotheistic world of 'natural theology'. The odd fact that there are no churches, temples, or religious rites and ceremonies, is simply part of the historical climate depicted".[62] Tolkien's works are pervaded by Christian thought, even though set in a pre-Christian world.[63]

The greatest Catholic Church theologian, Thomas Aquinas (thirteenth century), in his *Summa Theologiae*, tackles the

---

60. Lewis, C.S. *The Four Loves*. Op. cit., p. 115.
61. Except as a brief mention to "The One" in the appendices, in the context of the Fall of Númenor.
62. Tolkien, J.R.R., Carpenter, H. (Org.), Tolkien, C. (Assist.). *The Letters of J.R.R. Tolkien*. Op. cit., Letter 165, p. 220.
63. In *The Silmarillion* the chronology of Middle-earth is explained, which is divided in Ages: first, second and third. *The Lord of the Rings* is set in the Third Age, which then proceeds to the Fourth, Men's Age. Our present History is a continuation of that world Tolkien invented.

precise elements that Aristotle claimed constitute friendship:[64] *benevolence*, *reciprocity*, and *communication*, equivalent to the concept of communion. Antonin-Marcel Henry, who wrote the introductory remarks to "The Charity", explains: "the friendship love is founded upon a similarity in deed: I recognise in the other a similarity that creates between him and me a certain kind of 'communion', in the name of which I love".[65]

Christian friendship, which is based on charity, is intimate and personal, but not limited to selection and restriction. As remarked in the introduction to "The Charity":

> For St. Thomas, such a selective friendship represents a particular case of friendship. For him, as it was for Aristotle, friendship can be found wherever a community, *koinonia*,[66] can be found, this being understood as a group of people aiming at a common good, whether it be so indeed and later wanted together (the common good of the common blood), or whether it be simply wanted and decided together (an association).[67]

Thomas Aquinas supports Aristotle's theory that the friendship kind of love is based on reciprocal well-wishing, and that in such reciprocity dwells communion. Theology would, then, add to the philosophical truth: "since there is a communication between man and God, inasmuch as He communicates His happiness to us, some kind of friendship

---

64. In an introduction to Book V of the *Summa Theologiae*, Antonin-Marcel Henry explains that, in Greek, there were the verbs *philein* and *agapan*. *Philein* stands for a kind of affectionate love, while *agapan* described free choice. The noun *agape* was rarer, almost a coinage in the New Testament. In Latin, the *Vulgata* renders *philein* as *amare*, but *agapan* as *diligere*. "*Amare* is, therefore, the profound affection; *diligere*, the voluntary, deliberate and decided inclination" (2012, p. 287). The noun *agapè*, from *agapan*, is translated as *caritas* in Latin, a word that comes from *carus*, that is, dear, precious. "In the Christian language, the translation of *agapè bears all the senses of this word*, it becomes its equivalent, but to it is added the shade of esteem, 'of high esteem'" (Id.).

65. Quoted in Henry, Antonin-Marcel. "Introdução", in Aquino, Tomás de. *Suma Teológica*, Livro V. São Paulo: Loyola, 2012, p. 290.

66. Greek for communion.

67. Henry, Antonin-Marcel, T. *Suma Teológica*. Op. cit., p. 290.

must needs be based on this same communication".[68] This would happen from a supernatural point of view, not a physical one, because the human being is constituted by these two natures. The love based upon such communion is charity, a kind of friendship from Man to God, and from God to Man.

For the theologian, friendship could be characterised in two ways: as the love one feels for another one, or as the love one feels because of another person. Christian friendship focuses on the love one has for God, and the love one feels for one's fellow man because of it. The friendly kind of love has its source in the Divine Person, a source of love, and in the friend themselves; and loving the enemies is possible only because God, who, in Christian view, loves them unconditionally and grants to them the ability of reaching bliss, even though they still need to make use of free will to achieve it. The concept of fraternity, also, is universal and non-restrictive, because all Men are brothers before a single God, who is Father.

Aquinas emphasises the idea that friendship springs from self-love:[69] "just as unity is the principle of union, so the love with which a man loves himself is the form and root of friendship. For if we have friendship with others it is because we do unto them as we do unto ourselves".[70] It is necessary to bear in mind that such a self-directed good is based upon spiritual virtue, not on material goods.

Just as we saw in Aristotle, for Christian thought the good man is the one prone to friendship. Aquinas furthers this thought by claiming that love, whence friendship springs, must comply with three requirements: it must be *holy*, inasmuch as one loves another because of God; *just*, because it fulfils the needs of the other in goodness; and *true*, because it is really

---

68. Aquinas, T. *The Summa Theologica*. Translated by the Fathers of the English Dominican province. London: Catholic Way Publishing, 2014, SS, Q23, A1.
69. Such a reasoning has its bases on the Bible: "And thou shalt love the Lord thy God with all thine heart, and with all thy soul, and with all thy might" (Dt 6, 5). "This is the first and great commandment. And the second one is like unto it, Thou shalt love thy neighbor as thyself" (Matthew 22: 37-39), (Lv. 19, 18).
70. Aquinas, T. *The Summa Theologica*. Op. cit. SS, Q25, A5.

well-wishing and not self-seeking.

The wicked man, according to the Greek philosopher, can have ephemeral friendships based on profit or pleasure, but never perfect friendship, since it depends necessarily on goodness. Aquinas says: "The wicked have some share of self-love, in so far as they think themselves good. Yet such love of self is not true but apparent: and even this is not possible in those who are very wicked".[71] From a theological point of view, he complements this view by differentiating body and soul:

> Now the good look upon their rational nature or the inward man as being the chief thing in them, wherefore in this way they think themselves to be what they are. On the other hand, the wicked reckon their sensitive and corporeal nature, or the outward man, to hold the first place. Wherefore, since they know not themselves aright, they do not love themselves aright, but love what they think themselves to be. But the good know themselves truly, and therefore truly love themselves.
>
> [...] charity loves with greater fervour those who are united to us than those who are far removed; and in this respect the love of friends, considered in itself, is more ardent and better than the love of one's enemy.[72]

As for Lessing's critique — and, by extension, Hannah Arendt's — of love being coupled up with fraternity, such a claim cannot be observed in Aquinas, and is not observable in Rousseau's individualistic bourgeois view either: "Nor does it matter whether we say "neighbour," or "brother" according to 1 Jn. 4:21, or "friend," according to Lev. 19:18, because all these words express the same affinity", affirms the theologian.[73] Such affinity cannot be applied to the strictly political view; rather, the religious universe would provide a fraternal affinity among creatures destined to the divine bliss.

---

71. Id., SS, Q25, A7.
72. Id., SS, Q25, A7 and Q27, A7.
73. Id., SS, Q44, A7.

Friendship in Justice

In friendship according to charity one finds its most complete definition, since, for Aristotle, the knowledge of friendship happens through the object of love. According to Lewis, friendship is one of the four loves, and charity is nothing less than the virtue of Christian love. Thus, friendship and charity are the two loves least connected to senses, that is, the least "necessary" for our survival. They are not necessary for the body, being unable to generate or maintain life, but they are both particularly interconnected, and essential for the health of the soul.

On the other hand, we cannot talk about friendship without also talking about justice. According to Aristotle, this would be a complete virtue because not only does it benefit those who exercise it, but also the ones who receive it. Friendship, which always requires more than one person to exist, favours the occurrence of justice. By looking at things that way, one descries friendship in its public, political sphere.

Resuming our first hypothesis about *The Lord of the Rings*, that the final objective of the central plot is peace in Middle-earth brought about by the destruction of the Ring, and that this could not happen with a single individual but only with a group of people sharing one objective, we can conclude that friendship favours justice not only from an individual, but mainly from a collective point of view.

In the *Summa Theologiae* one also finds this direct relationship between the part and the whole, both equally necessary:

> Justice, as stated above [...] directs man in his relations with other men. Now this may happen in two ways: first as regards his relation with individuals, secondly as regards his relations with others in general, in so far as a man who serves a community, serves all those who are included in that community. [...] so that all acts of virtue can pertain to justice, in so far as it directs man to the common good.[74]

---

74. Aquinas, T. *The Summa Theologica*. Op. cit. SS, Q58, A5.

As for the definition of justice, the theologian explains:

> "Justice is a habit whereby a man renders to each one his due by a constant and perpetual will": and this is about the same definition as that given by the Philosopher (Ethic. v, 5) who says that "justice is a habit whereby an accordance".[75]

Aristotle claims that the worst man is that who does evil not only to himself, but also to his friends, while the best of men is that who, more than doing good to himself, also exercises virtue towards the others. We have seen that, despite the flaws in the heroes of *The Lord of the Rings*, the eucatastrophic ending happened mostly because each of them put his own self aside and accepted the challenge of embracing the common good. All of them could have run away from pain and peril, but each one showed courage and generosity in the name of justice and peace for Middle-earth and their friends.

Friendship, based in equality through virtue, requires reciprocity, as we have seen. We venture to say that friendship is the justice of love, which, in a certain way, requires from the other something in return — even an immaterial good like benevolence — reciprocity in well-wishing, so that friendship can be made real.

Based upon Book V of *The Nicomachean Ethics*, which deals precisely with the issue of justice, Thomas Aquinas equates justice and charity:

> Hence the Philosopher says (Rhet. i, 9): "The greatest virtues must needs be those which are most profitable to other persons, because virtue is a faculty of doing good to others. For this reason the greatest honours are accorded the brave and the just, since bravery is useful to others in warfare, and justice is useful to others both in warfare and in time of peace."[76]

Aquinas describes friendship, in the sense of 'affability', the virtue of making relations with others pleasant, and

---

75. Id., SS, Q58, A1.
76. Id., SS, Q58, A12.

because of that, he considers friendship equivalent to justice, even though, in this sense, it "yet it falls short of the notion of justice, because it lacks the full aspect of debt, whereby one man is bound to another".[77] However, the kind of friendship dealt with in this work is that associated to charity, more than simply affability. The latter, removed from the benevolent representation of charity, is linked to accidental friendship, based on pleasure, and not to the honest or perfect one, which occurs with reciprocal benevolence.

Therefore, a virtuous man's friendship is, for us, strictly connected to the love that generates justice, aiming at the common good. The choice for *The Nicomachean Ethics* leads us to a study about the ends of Man (and, by extension, the ends of the characters to be studied), having as the ultimate end the *eudaimonia*, that is, happiness (or bliss, according to the Christian view). Friendship is virtue or implies virtue, the necessary condition for the good that seeks no other end.

Within Tolkien's work, friendship is a tool that enables one to reach the ultimate end of the saga: destroying the One Ring and, consequently, conquering one's weaknesses which are potentialised by the magical object, achieving peace for himself and the free peoples of Middle-earth.

Magic: on, through and beyond the screen

Tolkien's *legendarium* is multiple in landscapes, fauna, flora, languages, architecture, and other natural and cultural variations. One of the places that catches our attention the most in Middle-earth is Lothlórien, an elvish kingdom resembling the gardens of Lórien in the Undying Lands, where Irmo, the Vala known as master of visions and dreams, dwells. Lothlórien stands as a timeless space in Middle-earth, and a place of resistance against Sauron's wicked deeds. Legolas, the elf in *The Fellowship of the Ring*, describes the place as such:

---

77. Aquinas, T. *The Summa Theologica*. Op. cit., SS, Q114, A2.

That is the fairest of all the dwellings of my people. There are no trees like the trees of that land. For in the autumn their leaves fall not, but turn to gold. Not till the spring comes and the new green opens do they fall, and then the boughs are laden with yellow flowers; and the floor of the wood is golden, and golden is the roof, and its pillars are of silver, for the bark of the trees is smooth and grey.[78]

It is not hard to understand why the image of a place like that can be so distinct for each mind that reads this description. Exactly because it is focused on such a detailed Secondary World, the movie adaptation of a work of fantasy can cause some strangeness to those readers most attached to the literary text, staunch defenders of the concept of fidelity in its adaptations.

Besides directing the movies that, along with Tolkien's literary works, will also be analysed here, Peter Jackson wrote part of the screenplay of the movie trilogy *The Lord of the Rings* (released from 2001 to 2003) with his wife Fran Walsh and Philippa Boyens, an assiduous reader of the book.

In the interviews found in the extended DVD versions of the movies, Jackson explains that he and Fran Walsh first transformed the three volumes into a ninety-page screenplay. Later, they showed the result to Boyens, who then started believing that it was possible to make a movie out of Tolkien's work, even though many captive readers of *The Lord of the Rings* such as herself were still sceptical about the successful completion of this transposition. That is due to the complexity of the work and its fantastic universe, which stimulates the personal creativity of each reader in such a way that leaves him or her less sympathetic to ideas different from those imagined by him or herself.

According to the screenwriters and the actors themselves, who were consulted for many scenes during the production of the screenplay, the plot of the movie was rewritten on a daily basis, with the book always within reach: the screenplay would always return to Tolkien's narrative. Despite that, we know

---

78. Tolkien, J.R.R. *The Lord of the Rings*. Op. cit., pp. 435-436.

that there are many discrepancies from one work to the other, especially because they are distinct artistic languages: each work of art gives to the contemporary audience its contribution to the same story.

It is important to emphasise, once more, that the intention here is not to categorise the works as "better" or "worse", nor to be overly attached to the concept of fidelity between movies and book. We see in them two versions of the same story, which acquire self-sufficient and distinct lives in each aesthetic category.

As we see it, evidently, the filmic adaptation should capture essential elements of the original work, otherwise it would be unfair to call it an "adaptation" had the screenwriters been irresponsible or even dishonest enough to disrespect the plot and the original concepts. This did not happen to *The Lord of the Rings* movies. Likewise, it is evident that we do not want to take away from Tolkien the merit of his noticeable creative intelligence and his arduous work as a writer, researcher, and professor. The intention is simply to give due importance to other artistic manifestation that have their own language and can inform and move in their own way.

The focus is not to verify what was lost from one version to the other, but to assess, without blind critical analysis, what is gained in the filmic adaptation. "Complete originality is not possible, nor desirable. [...] Within a wide and inclusive world of images and simulation, the adaptation becomes simply another text, taking part in a long discourse continuum."[79] From this perspective, we can consider the book and the movies of *The Lord of the Rings* independent works of art in conversation.

The adaptation of the work

In his essay *On Fairy-stories*, Tolkien criticised the representation of fairy-stories by means of images. "In human

---

79. Stam, R. "Teoria e Prática da Adaptação: da fidelidade à intertextualidade". *Ilha do Desterro*, Florianópolis, n. 51, p. 19-53, jul./dez. 2006, p. 23.

art Fantasy is a thing best left to words, to true literature",[80] he said. For him, the visible presentation of fantastic image, in painting, is "technically too easy", with the frequent result of silliness or morbidity. Hence the supposition, by some Tolkienists, that Tolkien would not have liked Jackson's movie adaptation, had he been alive to watch it, even though he had, in 1969, sold the rights of *The Hobbit* and *The Lord of the Rings* to United Artists due to the financial relief that the purchase would bring to his family.

On the other hand, it is worth saying that human beings naturally express their fantastic (sub)creations, whether it be by visual or performing arts. It is as though we are compelled to concretise our desires by means of imagic art, just like we do by means of words in literature.

It is certain that our thoughts can comprehend the enormous creative capacity of our minds, and that transferring it to the visual arts is only one fragment of this grandiosity. But it is also worth saying that such fragments favour — in this case, through the specificities of cinema — the awakening of other issues that lie dormant in the island of our desires, in a different way from that which literature grants us. Béla Balázs makes a claim that conforms to this observation: "A more important and decisive historical novelty was the fact that cinema did not show other things, but the same, only in a different way".[81]

Tolkien, in turn, believed that some representations of fairy-stories did not achieve "fantasy", mainly in theatrical plays, which rendered the representation of fantastic elements in a far-fetched way, not convincing at all. However, the advances in computer graphics might have made him reconsider. In the book *Lendo as Imagens do Cinema* [*Reading Movie Image*], Laurent Jullier and Michel Marie call the attention to the additions brought by new technologies to cinematographic productions and, thus, to the representations of fantastic

80. Tolkien, J.R.R. 'On Fairy-stories', in *Tree and Leaf*. Op. cit., p. 49.
81. Xavier, I. (org.). *A Experiência do Cinema*. Rio de Janeiro: Edições Graal, 1983, p. 84.

images. "The 'image synthesis' allows the contrivance of fantastic creatures so convincingly that *science fiction* rises from second class and genre film to the realm of the great in the global market".[82]

Emília Valente Galvão also brings a different, but not contrary to Tolkien's, observation:

> The impression of reality is a phenomenon connected to traces of expression matter in cinematographic language [...]. Other languages, such as the written text, are incapable of producing the impression of reality. However, it would be a mistake to infer that they are incapable of producing a diegetic effect. Proof of that is the fact that reading a novel can convey a "world effect" as intense as the appreciation of a movie, or even more intense than that.[83]

Ronald Kyrmse argues in favour of Peter Jackson,[84] reminding us of the fact that the filmmaker is another reader and admirer of Tolkien's trying to materialise his views about the Professor's work: "As a starting point, each of us has the right to our own view of Tolkien, and so does Peter Jackson. It is necessary to remember that he is also a fan of Tolkien, who loves his material and takes his work seriously."[85]

Kyrmse recollects Tolkien's impressions about an animated movie based on his work, expressed in a 1958 letter to the agent Forrest J. Ackerman. Tolkien criticised the proposed storyline because he believed it did not represent adequately "the heart of the tale". According to him, "the failure of poor films is often precisely in exaggeration, and in the intrusion of unwarranted matter owing to not perceiving where the core of

---

82. Jullier, L.; Marie, M. *Lendo as Imagens do Cinema*. São Paulo: Senac, 2009, p. 216.

83. Galvão, E.V. Ferramentas conceituais para um estudo da afetividade no cinema. *Interin*. Curitiba, v.15, n.1, 2013, pp. 163-174.

84. Concerning the adaptation of *The Lord of the Rings*. Kyrmse has been critical about *The Hobbit* film trilogy, but it had not been released when his book *Explicando Tolkien* was written.

85. Kyrmse, R. *Explicando Tolkien*. Op. cit., p. 141.

the original lies".[86]

For the author, the synopsis did not show respect to the dialogue, to the characterization, to the passage of time and to other issues. It is Kyrmse's — and my own — opinion that Jackson did not sin against the issues Tolkien raised, insofar as *The Lord of the Rings* is concerned.[87] "He might not have reproduced the letter of the book, but undoubtedly captured its spirit".[88]

That, it must be said, is not an opinion shared by Christopher Tolkien, J.R.R. Tolkien's third son and his literary executor. In a 2012 interview to *Le Monde*, Christopher shows his disapproval for the movies directed by Peter Jackson: "they have eviscerated the book, making it an action movie for 15- to 25-year-old young people", and "it seems that *The Hobbit* will be the same kind of movie".[89] According to Christopher, his father had been devoured by his own popularity and absorbed by the absurdities of the time we live in. He goes on to say that the "commercialization has reduced to nothing the aesthetic and philosophical impact of this creation. There is only one solution left for me: turning my head away".

Identification and Projection

As for the representations of friendship in *The Lord of the Rings* movie trilogy, we must first establish the basic concepts of *identification* and *projection* in the theory of the cinema according to the philosopher Edgar Morin. In his essay *The Cinema, or The Imaginary Man*, Morin talks about the soul of the cinema, and the processes that constitute its magic: *anthropomorphism*, which projects humanity in the exterior world; and *cosmomorphism*, which enables man to identify

---

86. Tolkien, J.R.R., Carpenter, H. (Org.), Tolkien, C. (Assist.). *The Letters of J.R.R. Tolkien*. Op. cit., Letter 210, p. 270.

87. *The Hobbit* trilogy, again, is the subject of other discussions.

88. Kyrmse, R. *Explicando Tolkien*. Op. cit., p. 144.

89. *The Hobbit* trilogy had not yet been released back in 2012.

with the exterior world. Nothing could be more adequate than using such artifices in fantasy movies.

Based on historical and psychological criticism, Morin explains that our projections interfere in our world perception. This leads us to believe that, in audiovisual representations that somehow deal with affectivity, it is necessary to awaken the spectators' emotions, passions, and feelings, so that they be able to project themselves onto the other, on the characters that appear before them.

Different from the scenes portraying the Eros kind of love, which can easily arouse our feelings and passions, the Friendship kind of love has the arduous task of winning the spectators by means of its milder, non-sexual affection. But it is paramount that the audience not only assimilate the elements of the movie in their inner world: they must also lend something to the fictional world portrayed. Within the concept of projection, Morin points out some stages involving this phenomenon: *automorphism*, when we attribute our tendencies to the others; *anthropomorphism*, when we transfer tendencies or traits of human characters to other beings or things, and, finally, in a superior level, *doubling*, which projects our own individual being into that which we contemplate. "In a way, anthropomorphism and doubling are moments where projection crosses over into alienation: these are magical moments".[90]

In contrast, the spectators can absorb the world presented to them so that identification takes place. "Identification with the world can broaden into cosmomorphism, where man feels and believes himself to be a microcosm".[91] Such phenomena occur reciprocally, man projects themself on the screen and identifies with it: the movie moves the spectator and, from then on, they tell the story together.

Projection and identification are never severed; one generates the other simultaneously. "Already the most banal

---

90. Morin, Edgar. *The Cinema, or the Imaginary Man.* Translated by Lorraine Mortimer. Minneapolis, London: University of Minnesota Press, 2005, p. 86.
91. Idem.

'projection' onto another — the 'I am putting myself in his place' — is an identification of myself with him that facilitates and calls for the identification of him with me: he has become assimilable".[92]

Just like Tolkien explains that fantasy is present in the Secondary World, that onto which our desires are projected, Morin couples up magic and dream: "the magical universe is subjective vision that believes itself to be real and objective".[93] Likewise, subjectivity is necessary for the existence of magic: the one generates, feeds, sustains, and prolongs the other.

The subjects who are the spectators of the movies based on Tolkien's fantasy, and the readers as well, carry within them a microcosm of their own dreams: a world in which a wizard guides them, in which evil has a name and a place to be fought, a world which has a Shire full of trees and calmness awaiting them in a eucatastrophic ending. It is not difficult, thus, to assimilate a representation of friendship: the heroes' friends (whose flaws are similar to the spectators') are, therefore, their friends too. The spectator and the character become attuned, friendship springs up in our imagination, and it starts dwelling with us, in a way, as factually as it happens with our friends in the Primary World.

Magic, according to Morin, consists of a preobjective vision of the world, as well as of a presubjective phase of our affectivity flow. Thus, our affectivity succeeds the concretization of our dreams. We forget ourselves and enter the imaginary universe of the screens – there is a reciprocal giving between ourselves and the projected scenes, making magic happen. But we cannot stay in that phase for long, and we end up realising how distant we are from fantastic reality: magic, then, leaves a mark on us, and gives back affection as a proof of its existence.

"The zone of affective participation is that of mixed, uncertain, ambivalent projection-identifications. [...] In this zone, neither magic nor subjectivity is manifest and

92. Idem.
93. Id., p. 87.

latent".[94] According to Morin, love is the supreme projection-identification and, as we have seen, friendship is a form of love. Therefore, its representation consists of this interplay between projection-identification-magic-affectivity.

Such issues also apply to the relationship between the reader and the book, not only to the spectator and the movie. In cinematographic language, however, one finds visual elements that render the projection-identification process more marked and slightly imposed. Thus, all the elements that constitute cinema language — composition, art direction (makeup and costume design), cinematography, and others — in the end contribute to impress the spectators in a more immediate way than books normally do.

> The costume (that disguise), the face (that mask), the talk (those conventions), the feeling of our own importance (that comedy), maintain in ordinary life this spectacle offered to self and others — that is, imaginary projection-indentifications.[95]

According to Marcel Martin, cinema is both an art and a language. An art because it has been providing original creations since its beginnings, as exemplified by the illusionist master George Méliès, and it is language because it brings the distinct writing of each producer, with their own style. In this sense, the cinematic image is almost magical inasmuch as "the camera creates something more than mere duplication of reality".[96]

For Martin, image is the basic element of cinematographic language and has its own characteristics. He claims that the filmic aesthetic carries an affective value, since reality as it is presented on the screen is the product of the director's subjective perception. Quoting Henri Angel and Morin, Martin says that:

---

94. Morin, Edgar. *The Cinema, or the Imaginary Man.* Op. cit., p. 89.
95. Id., p. 91. Emphasis by the author.
96 . Martin, M. *A Linguagem Cinematográfica*. São Paulo: Brasiliense, 2011, p. 15.

[…] cinema is *intensity, intimacy, ubiquity*: intensity because the filmic image, especially the foreground,[97] has an almost magical force which offers an absolutely specific view of the real, and because the music, with its sensorial and lyric role, at the same time reinforces the penetration power of image; intimacy because the image (again through the foreground) makes us literally penetrate the beings (by means of their faces, open books to the souls) and the things; ubiquity, finally, because cinema carries us freely in space and time, because it condenses time (everything feels longer on the screen) and above all because it recreates the very duration, allowing the movie to flow without discontinuity in the stream of your personal conscience.[98]

Elements such as framing, planes of action (such as the foreground emphasised in the quotation above), angles, and camera movement constitute the expressivity of the image. The *framing* is the boundary the camera establishes to the reality it wants to show; the *plane of action* refers to the distance between the camera and the object; the *angle* corresponds to the position of the camera before the filmed object; and *camera movement* has to do with the direction through which the camera moves from one point to another. All of this is governed by an intention, which can convey, for instance, more expressivity, drama, rhythm, and impact to the screen.

However, it is *film editing*, according to Martin, which is the most specific element of cinematographic language: "*the organization of the planes of action in a movie in certain conditions and order of duration*".[99] The selection of what will be shown and how this will be done happens in an editing station, where the art of film editing takes place. It has the force of a psychological mechanism inducing the human mind to complete a message owing to a succession of planes edited in such a way so as to give us the impression of real perception. "We can assume that the succession of planes in a movie is

97. Short distance from the camera enabling to show a person or object more closely.
98. Martin, M. *A Linguagem Cinematográfica*. Op. cit., p. 25. Emphasis by the author.
99. Id., p. 147. Emphasis by the author.

founded on the *outlook* or on the *thought* [...] of the characters
or the spectator".[100]

All these artifices contribute, as we said before, to the
resurrection and transmutation of magic by the work of fiction,
as suggested by Edgar Morin. As all other aesthetic productions,
it feeds (and feeds on) the deepest and most intense affective
manifestations. "Cinema is precisely this symbiosis: a system
that tends to integrate the spectator to the flow of the movie.
*A system that tends to integrate the flow of the movie to the
psychic flow of the spectator*".[101]

The engagement of the spectator's self with the characters
can occur either with the hero or the villain, by similarity or
contrast: their characteristics may conform to what we live,
and identification may be direct, or they might arouse other
passions, even in an unruly way, whether or not we ethically
agree with them or are even conscious of them.

The way movies are communicated and experienced
also favours spectators' projection and identification. Lights
off, all seats facing the screen, the absolute silence required
of the audience: everything configures an exclusive and
individual experience. According to Hugo Mauherhofer, the
"cinematographic experience offers plausible material for
the fantasies and dreams nourished by countless people".[102]
Because of that, the passive spectators, if they do not keep
enough distance, will allow little room for critical thinking. On
the other hand, such distance might also impair the enjoyment
that comes from the engagement between spectator and fantasy.

Wondrous stories, as we have seen, bring benefits such as
fantasy, recovery, escape, and consolation, not only in literary
language, but also in other aesthetic categories such as cinema.
If we join the themes of fantastic literature and the power of

---

100. Martin, M. *A Linguagem Cinematográfica*. Op. cit., p. 155. Emphasis by the
author.
101. Id., p. 125. Emphasis by the author.
102. Xavier, I. (org.). *A Experiência do Cinema*. Rio de Janeiro: Edições Graal,
1983, p. 378.

magic and engagement of the cinematographic universe, we can understand why the public is so charmed and eager for the experience with the Secondary World, both in pages and screen.

In the cinematographic portrayals of friendship, we will try to show how the producers of the movies sought, above all, to awaken our affections that arise from the magic of the cinema. Such magic can only take place with the participation of our own dreams, the desires that feed the Secondary World, like the yearning to find friends that walk alongside us towards the heroic journeys of our personal and collective challenges.

Chapter Three

Corruption and division:
the self, the double and the other

We will now focus on the thought-provoking and probably most complex character Tolkien created: Gollum. To do that, we will turn to the representation of the *self* as the subject, who engages with themselves, and will see how this is reflected in their relationship with the other.

What immediately catches our attention in Gollum is, undoubtedly, his conflicted, unstable, dichotomic personality: two persons existing in a single being, in perpetual discord. But it has not been always like that. It is known that Gollum is a creature closely related to a Hobbit and that, originally, he was known as Sméagol.[1] In the first book of the saga, Gandalf tells how that came to happen when he explains to Frodo how the Ring ended up in Sméagol's hand:

> [Sméagol] was interested in roots and beginnings; he dived into deep pools; he burrowed under trees and growing plants; he tunnelled into green mounds; and he ceased to look up at the hill-tops, or the leaves on trees, or the flowers opening in the air: his head and his eyes were downward.[2]

The way the character is presented, showing his interest in subterranean matters, is a metaphor of his own personality: Sméagol was a self-absorbed creature, with a gloomy, curious mind, searching for his origins (roots) and progressively more

---

1. Sméagol is a translation of the name Trahald, in Westron, the common language of Men. The etymological root of Sméagol is the Old English *smeagan*, meaning 'to investigate'.

2. Tolkien, J.R.R. *The Lord of the Rings*. London: HarperCollins, 2008, p. 69.

interested in lowly matters, ignoring that which elevated him.

We notice that his characteristics shift in a descending manner: "he ceased to look up at the hill-tops, or the leaves on trees, or the flowers opening in the air: his head and his eyes were downward". That explains why, as we will see, he was easy prey for the power of Sauron's magical object: his mind and body, bent to low, vile things, were prone to the malign forces of the One Ring, a controlling and corrupting object.

One day, Sméagol went fishing in the Gladden Fields with Déagol, a friend similar to him, probably part of the same family. When he noticed that his friend had found the Ring in the river, Sméagol instantly desired the object and, seeing that Déagol would not surrender it, without thinking much, Sméagol strangled him, giving Déagol no chance of defence.[3]

It is possible to affirm that the power of the Ring played a role in that murder, because the evil object would bring forth the darkest side in people, awakening the desire of domination. But it cannot be denied that Sméagol's previous choices, such as his way of living and his worldview, contributed significantly for the power of the Ring to manifest so fast in him. Totally possessed by the object, Gollum brought about his own unhappiness, full of hatred, not least for the Ring itself: "He hated it and loved it, as he hated and loved himself".[4]

Whoever keeps a Great Ring, according to Gandalf, "'does not die, but he does not grow or obtain more life, he merely continues, until at last every minute is a weariness'".[5] Attracted by the magical object, which could make its user disappear, Sméagol spent a long time invisible and, when he was visible, he was unpleasant. Banned from his community, his inner personality, which we can call his 'double', got stronger to the point of changing his physical appearance.

Déagol's murder looks back to the biblical narrative of Cain

3. Unlike Peter Jackson's movie (*The Return of the King*), in which a strife ensues before Sméagol strangling Déagol.
4. Tolkien, J.R.R. *The Lord of the Rings*. Op. cit., p. 73.
5. Id., p. 61.

and Abel, sons of Adam and Eve. Cain killed his brother out of envy. Just like him who wanted Abel's favour before God, Sméagol wanted what his friend held in his hands: the Ring of Power; and, just like Cain killed Abel to assuage his greed, Sméagol kills Déagol. After the fratricide, Cain was banned from the community, and the effect of the Ring also made Sméagol very unpopular among his peers, so that he became more and more isolated.

The Precious

Before proceeding in the Sméagol-Gollum analysis, it is important to know more about the meaning of the One Ring: after all, both the magical object and Gollum appeared almost simultaneously in Tolkien's mind. The writer made them public in *The Hobbit* (1937), his first published book, initially told to amuse his children.

At first, the Ring was a simple magical object in a fantastic story, with the power of making invisible anyone who used it — as well as the user's clothes and everything he or she was holding. Bilbo Baggins, a Hobbit, found the Ring in a very dark cave, when he got lost from his Dwarf friends, as told in the chapter "Riddles in the Dark": "It was a turning point in his career, but he did not know it. He put the ring in his pocket almost without thinking..."[6]

However, the author's creative process regarding the mythical value of the Ring took many years to become complete. When Tolkien wrote about the Ring for the first time in *The Hobbit,* he did not know yet about its history and its value that we now understand through *The Lord of the Rings.*

Even though the Ring was said to be a "turning point in his career", everything it does for Bilbo in *The Hobbit* is to help him overcome problems by making him invisible. By then, the author had no idea of the Ring's origins nor of what it would

---

6. Tolkien, J.R.R. *The Hobbit*. London: HarperCollins, 2006, p. 81.

become in further narratives. Only later, while writing *The Lord of the Rings* as a continuation to *The Hobbit*, as requested by Allen & Unwin, did Tolkien suggest to the publishing house some changes in the plot of *The Hobbit*, particularly in the aforementioned chapter "Riddles in the Dark" — which deals exactly with Bilbo's finding of the Ring and his encounter with Gollum — so that both stories became more cohesive. The second edition of *The Hobbit* was published in 1951, three years before the launch of *The Lord of the Rings*.[7]

Later, in the same chapter, we are introduced to Gollum in that dark place. This is how the narrator presents him:

> Deep down here by the dark water lived old Gollum, a small slimy creature. I don't know where he came from, nor who or what he was. He was Gollum—as dark as darkness, except for two big round pale eyes in his thin face. [...] He was looking out of his pale lamp-like eyes for blind fish, which he grabbed with his long fingers as quick as thinking. He liked meat too. Goblin he thought good, when he could get it; but he took care they never found him out.[8]

The origin of his moniker is explained in *The Hobbit* too: "And when he said *gollum* he made a horrible swallowing noise in his throat. That is how he got his name, though he always called himself 'my precious'".[9]

We will see that the "precious", in the second edition of *The Hobbit*, is not exactly — or not exclusively — Gollum, but the

7. The edition of *The Hobbit* used in this book follows the 1951 text. In the 1937 version, Bilbo found the Ring in the goblins' cave, where Gollum dwelt, and, by winning the riddle contest against the vile creature, his reward was the piece of information that would enable him to get out of the cave. At first, Gollum wanted to give him the Ring as a reward, but Bilbo had already found it and did not tell him he had it. On the second edition, more compatible with *The Lord of the Rings*, Bilbo escapes with the Ring unbeknown to Gollum: in a seemingly fortuitous event, he puts his hand in his pocket trying to escape the goblins, accidentally puts the Ring and becomes invisible.

8. Tolkien, J.R.R. *The Hobbit.* Op. cit., pp. 84-85.

9. Id., p. 86.

Ring which he calls his "birthday-present".[10] He calls himself "precious", as he calls the magical object also. This is already a hint of the "double" apparent in that strange creature: the Ring is, in a certain way, Gollum's "double", that into which he transformed. Paradoxically, he ended up possessed by the object that promises him power.

Jean-Pierre Vernant, in *Myth and Thought among the Greeks*, explains "how the Greeks gave a visible form to certain powers of the beyond belonging to the realm of the invisible".[11] To do so, he used as an example the *kolossos*, which, according to custom, were objects (normally erected stones, whether or not in the shape of a statue) which substituted for an absent corpse.[12]

According to Vernant, "The kolossos is not an image; it is a 'double', as the dead man is a double of his living self".[13] His concept of the double is close to the "Uncanny" proposed by Freud in his 1919 essay "Das Unheimliche". Vernant goes on:

> A double is completely different from an image. [...] For the person who sees it, the double is an external reality, but one whose peculiar character, in its very appearance, sets it in opposition to familiar objects and to the ordinary surroundings of life. It exists simultaneously on two contrasting planes: just when it shows itself to be present, it also reveals itself as not of this world and as belonging to some other, inaccessible sphere.[14]

Even though not a vertical, static monument, the Ring brings some functions attributed to the *kolossos* to those who wear it for a long time, as it happens with Gollum: being an

---

10. Tolkien, J.R.R. *The Hobbit.* Op. cit., p. 95.

11. Vernant, Jean-Pierre. *Myth and Thought among the Greeks.* New York: Zone Books, 2006, p. 321.

12. Tolkien's "Argonath" are good examples referring back to the concept of *kolossos*, which etymologically "retains the idea of something erected, something that has been set up" (Vernant, 2006, p. 321). Both colossal statues represented the ancient kings of Gondor, Isildur and Anárion, and stood upon either side of River Anduin, in the northern border of Gondor.

13. Vernant, Jean-Pierre. *Myth and Thought among the Greeks.* Op. cit., p. 322.

14. Id., p. 325.

object that, as the kolossos, plays the role of "double" in that it encapsulates Gollum's *self*, who is a kind of Sméagol's "living corpse". As the *kolossos*, the Ring corresponds to a "peculiar and ambiguous presence that is also the sign of an absence";[15] and, thus, it steals Sméagol's life and gives voice to Gollum.

However, the Ring is not limited to making the "undead" visible, it also confers invisibility to its wearer, and, with time, the ones possessed by it lose indeed their physical form. Its power goes beyond: it corrupts all those who wield it, "the *kolossos*, as a double, always establishes a link between the living and the underworld".[16] Thus, the Ring pushes the person away from the virtuous path into the vicious one, if we are to use the Aristotelian concepts. Whoever surrenders to the Ring, by thirst for power and selfishness, ends up emptying oneself of the nobility of character, distancing oneself from the chief good, *eudaimonia*, happiness.

In Book 2 of Plato's *Republic* (IV BC), we find the legend of the Ring of Gyges. That is a ring that granted Gyges invisibility and favoured his moral corruption. With the magical object, he would be able to make morally dubious decisions without being seen. Plato invites us to "imagine two men, one just, the other unjust, given full license to do whatever they like, and then follow them to observe where each will be led by his desires".[17] With this myth, we see that justice is connected to the concept of truth.

We can safely affirm that those with a noble character have nothing to hide, and, therefore, do not choose to be invisible. In Tolkien's work, on the other hand, we see that even the most virtuous can err. That is why we see, for instance, that Gandalf and Galadriel are afraid of the Ring, and that the virtuous Hobbit Frodo gives in at the end of his journey, failing to throw the Ring in the fires of Mount Doom and deciding to keep it.

---

15. Id., p. 323.
16. Id., p. 327.
17. Plato. *The Republic*. Translated by F.M. Cornford. Oxford: at the Clarendon Press, 1955, p. 43.

Maria do Rosário Ferreira Monteiro points out that Sauron's Ring, as a mandala, symbolises the Universal Self[18] and she quotes Timothy O'Neil:

> The ring is perfect and stands for the Self — The Ruling Ring [...] is the way in which the archetype of the Self-in-potentia personifies himself [...].
> The form and function of the Ring are not left in doubt. The Ring's fate is etched inside and out in fiery letters: "*One Ring to rule them all, One Ring to find them. One Ring to bring them all and in the darkness bind them.*"[19]

At first, Gollum does not realise that Bilbo has the Ring, but he does notice his presence in the dark cave and soon wants to devour him. When the Hobbit notices the strange creature there, both of them start to talk and, were it not for Gollum's curiosity in knowing the origin of Bilbo's elvish sword, Sting, he would have devoured Bilbo at that very moment.

Intending to find out more about the sword, and to look friendly, Gollum proposes that he and Bilbo play a game of riddles. The Hobbit, also curious about that being, accepts it, and the game starts with Gollum formulating the first riddle. To the strange creature's surprise, *The Hobbit* solves it very easily. And Gollum replies:

> "It must have a competition with us, my preciouss! If precious asks, and it doesn't answer, we eats it, my preciousss. If it asks us, and we doesn't answer, then we does what it wants, eh? We shows it the way out, yes!"[20]

And so is configured the myth of the Theban Sphynx in

---

18. Monteiro, M.R.F. *J.R.R. Tolkien The Lord of the Rings: A Viagem e a Transformação.* 1992. Master's thesis, Universidade Nova de Lisboa. She is referring to the Jungian concept of the Self: "As for the trilogy [*sic*] *The Lord of the Rings*, the constellated archetype lying on its base is precisely that which, according to Jung, occupies a central position in the "geography" of human *psyche* — the Self (*Selbst*)" (p. 64).
19. 1979, O'Neil, quoted in Monteiro. Id., p. 84, emphasis added by Monteiro.
20. Tolkien, J.R.R. *The Hobbit.* Op. cit., p. 87.

Tolkienian narrative: either Mr. Baggins answers the riddle of that repulsive creature or he would be, literally, devoured. The competition started relatively easy for both, but, in time, it grew more difficult, particularly for Bilbo, who had the disadvantage of being afraid of becoming a meal unless he answered correctly.

In his article "*O Senhor dos Anéis* e o Mal: Corrupção, virtudes e Deus" [*The Lord of the Rings* and Evil: Corruption, virtues and God], Diego Klautau[21] speaks from a theological point of view to interpret this episode and its outcome: "It is luck that made Bilbo find the One Ring while Gollum was looking for it. It was luck that allowed Bilbo to win the riddle contest and take the Ring away".[22] Klautau associates, based on St. Augustine's ideas, luck (as "chance" and "fate") to divine providence — Eru Ilúvatar, in that case — "which allows those who search for and have the Grace of remaining in virtue to unite and act against those who deviate from the path of Goodness".[23]

If we put these two concepts — providence and grace — sequentially, we understand that divine providence is not dependent so much on the heroes' merits that come from the practice of virtue, but is, rather, an aid that drives them, with the gift of Grace, through the path of virtuous action so that they can have a happy ending (*eucatastrophic*) in their journey.

After that riddle, Bilbo had to formulate a final question to Gollum, which would decide the winner of the game. To intimidate him, the creature sits close to Bilbo, who, desperate, starts fidgeting with his belongings, looking for an idea: "'What have I got in my pocket?' he said aloud. He was talking to himself, but Gollum thought it was a riddle, and he was frightfully upset.'[24]

21. Klautau, D. "*O Senhor dos Anéis* e o Mal: Corrupção, virtudes e Deus", *Revista Ciências da Religião*, 2008, 6, 1, pp. 90-124.
22. Id., p. 99.
23. Ibid..
24. Tolkien, J.R.R. *The Hobbit*. Op. cit., pp. 92-93.

Gollum was not able to discover what Bilbo had in his pocket because he would frequently keep his precious in a rock in his island, and so he lost the game. Even then, because of his evil nature, he did not show Bilbo the way out (differently from what happens in the first edition), but he started to worry about the whereabouts of the Ring, since he could not find it in its hiding-place. Still by luck — or, rather, Providence — the Ring slipped into Bilbo's finger who, without realising it, became invisible and finally — though not without further difficulties — managed to escape from there.

The origins of the Ring

Before the foreword to *The Lord of the Rings* we find the famous poem about the Rings of Power. The lines "One Ring to rule them all, One Ring to find them, / One Ring to bring them all and in the darkness bind them" are engraved in the magical object devised by Sauron, written in the Black Speech of Mordor. When he forged the Ring, the Enemy became dependent on it, because he transferred to it part of his vital power. The Dark Lord's objective was to create a domination weapon but, paradoxically, it also dominated him, because the destruction of the Ring would also entail the definitive loss of his physical form. The Ring acted in a similar way with everyone, in a higher or lesser degree according to the person's strength and wisdom, and the amount of time the person spent with the object.

The origin of the Ring dates to c.1600 of the Second Age of Tolkien's universe, while its destruction happened in 3019 of the Third Age, so it existed for about 4860 years.

The First Age comprises 450 years of the Trees (which are equivalent to 4312 solar years) — in a time when the sun and the moon did not exist, and the land of the Valar was illuminated by the Two Trees —, plus 590 solar years, after the creation of the sun and the moon.

See the following table for the exact dates:

First Age	4902 years
Second Age	3441 years
Third Age	3021 years
Fourth Age	The age of Men, coinciding with History in the Primary World

The Maia Sauron, Morgoth's lieutenant, after the downfall of his master, tried to seduce the Elves, presenting himself in a guise of beauty and wisdom, using the name "Annatar". Even though not wholly trusted by the Elves, he found among the elven-smiths of Eregion an opportunity to teach his abilities and lure them into forging Rings of Power, and so the Elves made many rings. "But secretly Sauron made One Ring to rule all the others", as stated in *The Silmarillion*.[25] The Elves, however, realised the trap and fled, managing to preserve three of the rings they had produced. The rest of them Sauron took for himself and distributed to other peoples in Middle-earth: seven for the Dwarves and nine to Men, and "all those rings that he governed he perverted".[26]

After that, they spent some years under Sauron's dominion, the Dark Years, but he ended up being resisted by the Elves — who had taken refuge for some time — and by Men, particularly the Númenóreans. It is told in *The Silmarillion* that the Men of Númenor had such great power that

> the servants of Sauron would not withstand them, and hoping to accomplish by cunning what he could not achieve by force, he left Middle-earth for a while and went to Númenor as a hostage of Tar-Calion the King. And there he abode, until at the last by his craft he had corrupted the hearts of most of that people, and set them at war with the Valar, and so compassed their ruin [...].[27]

---

25. Tolkien, J.R.R. *The Silmarillion*. London: HarperCollins, 1999, p. 344.
26. Id., pp. 345-46.
27. Id., p. 347.

Some Númenóreans, under the lead of Elendil, whose sons were Isildur and Anárion, abandoned the island before its downfall, and established the kingdoms of Gondor and Arnor in Middle-earth. After nine years, Sauron attacked Gondor and fled. Thus was formed the Last Alliance of Elves and Men (led by Gil-galad and Elendil, respectively), in retaliation to Sauron's attacks who, by then, had assumed a terrible appearance, wearing his Ring and clothed in power.

The hosts of the Alliance, in the end, conquered their enemies in the battle of Dagorlad. Elendil and Gil-galad struck Sauron and died afterwards. Isildur, Elendil's son, cut the defeated Enemy's finger and kept the One Ring, and the Second Age came to an end.

Isildur was advised by the Elves Elrond and Círdan to throw the Ring in the fires of Orodruin, or Mount Doom, where it had been forged, but Elendil's heir refused to part with the object and wanted to keep it as a compensation for the death of his beloved ones, apart from considering it the proof of his victory over the Enemy. And the Ring he held had a most beautiful appearance, so he did not allow it to be destroyed. But keeping that object led him to an unfortunate fate, when a host of orcs attacked him and his people: "Then the Orcs saw him as he laboured in the stream, and they shot him with many arrows, and that was his end".[28]

The Ring, we notice, is able to reveal the level of corruption in the individual who bears or covets it: Isildur was vain and wanted to keep the malign object as a token of victory, crystallising his hatred towards the Enemy. The Númenórean was not looking for Good itself, but to display his vengeance, reinforcing the betraying character of the Ring: that is why the object forged by the Dark Lord was also known as 'Isildur's Bane'.

After 2461 years, in the River Anduin at the Gladden Fields, where Isildur had been defeated, Déagol found the Ring and was murdered by his friend Sméagol, Gollum.

---

28. Tolkien, J.R.R. *The Silmarillion*. Op. cit., p. 354.

Two names, no identity

The relationship between Sméagol and himself is crucial for us to understand his relationship with his double (Gollum) and the others — and, therefore, to understand how friendship manifested (or not) in him. We know that, in *The Nicomachean Ethics*, Aristotle highlights that the "Friendly relations to others, and all the characteristics by which friendship is defined, seem to be derived from our relations towards ourselves."[29]

Gollum's relation to himself, as we could notice, is wholly unstable. In fact, this comes from the fact that he lacks unity and, therefore, a single self cannot be identified in him. According to an article by Leif Jacobsen,[30] Sméagol/Gollum is both good and evil, or even neutral. It is an *a priori* truth, because in the outcome of the saga the character decides to keep the Ring – that is, he chooses Evil.

Gollum's character is not very clear in the narrative, and this can be exemplified through several moments of the book. We could highlight the moment when Frodo Baggins, following his path to Mordor to destroy the Ring, asks his friend Sam Gamgee: "It's my doom, I think, to go to that Shadow yonder, so that a way will be found. But will good or evil show it to me?".[31] We know that it is precisely Gollum who guided *The Hobbit* friends to their destination. Such ambiguity is seen also when Sam and Frodo, in a metalinguistic dialogue, reflect upon the kind of characters they could be — as though they were already part of a great story told to their descendants — and Sam says about Gollum: "I wonder if he thinks he's the hero or the villain?".[32]

---

29. Aristotle. *The Nicomachean Ethics*, trans. by F. H. Peters, 10 edn. London: Kegan Paul, Trench, Trübner & Co., 1906, p. 294.
30. Jacobsen, L. "The Undefinable Shadowland: A Study of the Complex Question of Dualism in J.R.R. Tolkien's *The Lord of the Rings*". Lund University, Sweden, 1997. <http://tolkiensarda.se/new/alster/shadowland.pdf> [Accessed 24 March, 2020].
31. Tolkien, J.R.R. *The Lord of the Rings*. Op. cit., p. 788.
32. Id., p. 933.

Gollum can be good insofar as the Ring would not have been destroyed without him. Moreover, he saves Frodo and Sam from perilous situations, in a way, such as when he protected them in the Dead Marshes, and even by helping them get to Mordor, where their Quest would be fulfilled.

But Gollum is also very cruel, not only when he sees the Ring in front of him and tries to snatch it, but also when he contrives an evil plan so that the terrible giant spider, Shelob, can attack Frodo. Unable to break the promise made upon the Ring — that he would not harm Frodo — Gollum thinks of a way to get his *precious* to himself without harming Frodo with his own hands: sending him into the lair of a powerful predator, hoping that she kills him, clearing the way for him to get the Ring.

Jacobsen also believes that he could be a neutral character because he serves no one: he is not a Sauron's servant nor does he follow the deliberations of the Council of Elron, which decided that the Ring must be destroyed. Gollum serves only himself, even though he does serve the power of the Ring, that is, he is dependent on his own desires, the Ring being a symbol of the self.

Such considerations are valid, but they make us reflect upon other, perhaps deeper, issues. Otto Rank, in his psychoanalytical study of the Double, calls the attention to the connection between this concept and the myth of Narcissus. The individual would be so centred in the ego that, in a paranoid state, he feels threatened by the destruction of it, thus generating another self, the double.[33]

We know that Narcissus was very attractive, the son of the river god Cephissus and the nymph called Liriope, and his life was promised to be long, provided he did not contemplate his own image — thus predicted the oracle. Desired by everyone, he one day attracted the nymph Echo, whom Hera, Zeus's spouse, punished by making her repeat the last words she heard. Feeling despised, Echo pined because of her unrequited

---

33. Rank, O. *Double: A Psychoanalytic Study*, translated by Harry Tucker Jr. Chapel Hill: The University of North Carolina Press, 1971, p. 83.

love, but her voice remained in the pool where she dwelled.

Other nymphs were rejected by Narcissus, and so they asked Nemesis, the goddess of fate and vengeance, to make Cephissus's son suffer the consequences of his arrogance. One day, Narcissus found himself in Echo's territory and, hearing his own words repeated by the nymph, he was anguished, unable to see her for whose words he fell in love. Determined to bathe in Echo's pool, he saw his own image, and fell in love with it. Desperate, because his love would not be reciprocated, he gradually lost his beauty and charm and eventually decayed there. In the place where he died there sprang a flower which bears his name.

Gollum, as we saw, was obsessed not only with lower things, but also with himself. His selfish character made him easy prey to the Ring, a malign symbol of power. With time, corrupted by the object, which fed even more his vanity and arrogance, he became more and more disfigured.

Self-absorbed, Gollum started to deny his origins and, with that, denied his own self. It is said in *The Hobbit* that "these ordinary above ground everyday sort of riddles were tiring for him. Also they reminded him of days when he had been less lonely and sneaky and nasty, and that put him out of temper".[34] This selfish characteristic of Gollum pushes him further away from what Aristotle considers essential for the man who displays perfect friendship: virtue, goodness, benevolence.

According to Otto Rank, the fear of the destruction of the ego comes from the fear of death, and the desire for immortality. Paradoxically, the existence of a double, which would, in principle, fight off this fear, leads to disgrace through suicide. Clément Rosset, in his *The Real and its Double*, claims: "what anguishes the subject, much more than his imminent death, is his non-reality, his non-existence".[35] Aristotle also has something to say:

34. Tolkien, J.R.R. *The Hobbit.* Op. cit., p. 89.
35. Rosset, C. *O Real e seu Duplo: Ensaio sobre a ilusão.* São Paulo: L&PM, 1988, p. 78.

for existence is good to the good i man. But it is for himself that each wishes the good; no one would choose to have all that is good (as e.g. God is in complete possession of the good).[36]

Faced with this deadlock, the most intriguing question remains: who is he? If we do not know who Gollum properly is, his true identity disappears: to serve his own self, in a selfish spiral, is the same as to serve no one.

Gollum and Sméagol are in permanent conflict, even as they depend on one another. The "I" disappears in his speech and is replaced by "we". In other circumstances, it is replaced by the third-person singular:

> Gollum was talking to himself. Sméagol was holding a debate with some other thought that used the same voice but made it squeak and hiss. A pale light and a green light alternated in his eyes as he spoke.
> 'Sméagol promised,' said the first thought.
> 'Yes, yes, my precious,' came the answer, 'we promised: to save our Precious, not to let Him have it – never. [...]'[37]

Note that the narrator normally refers to the character as Gollum. Frodo, however, calls him Sméagol. It is as though he tried all the time to rescue the creature's true personality, conferring dignity and respect by using his true name. The text, however, is clear in that Gollum's personality dominates Sméagol. As Rosset affirms:

> In the evil pair that unites the self to the phantasmatic other, the real is not on the other side of the self, but on the side of the phantasm: it is not the other that doubles myself, I myself am the double of the other.[38]

Gollum's dominion over his own identity is such that the moments in which Sméagol surfaces are something remarkable:

---

36. Aristotle. *The Nicomachean Ethics*. Op. cit., p. 295.
37. Tolkien, J.R.R. *The Lord of the Rings*. Op. cit., p. 827.
38. Rosset, C. *O Real e seu Duplo: Ensaio sobre a ilusão*. Op. cit., p. 78.

> For one thing, he noted that Gollum used I, and that seemed usually to be a sign, on its rare appearances, that some remnants of old truth and sincerity were for the moment on top.[39]

The effect of the Ring annihilates Gollum, emphasising the internal conflict he already had before finding it. Anguish is his permanent companion, who lays on the Ring all his salvation, when the object is, in fact, his bane. In this sense, Rank says the following about the phenomenon of double personality:

> The most prominent symptom of the forms which the double takes is a powerful consciousness of guilt which forces the hero no longer to accept the responsibility for certain actions of his ego, but to place it upon another ego, a double, who is either personified by the devil himself or is created by making a diabolical pact.[40]

Gollum is in constant search for the Ring, bearing the anguish of being nothing, of not existing, meaningless in life. The power of the Ring, apparently, possesses the seducer and the traitor: it empties the being of its existence inasmuch as it promises power over everything. Gollum, at times, seems to try returning to what he originally was, but fails.

Rosset shows two ways by which one can return to one's self: "the simple one, consisting of accepting the problem, and even rejoicing in it; and the complex one, which consists of refusing it, returning to it with interest, as the ancient stoic adage goes *fata volentem ducunt, nolentem trahunt*."[41]

Gollum drags himself. He does not accept who he was, nor does he accept who he is. This crisis reaches its climax when he meets Frodo in the fire chasm of Mount Doom, in Mordor, with the One Ring in his hands. In his most decisive moment, Gollum does not even think anymore. His annihilation, or rather Sméagol's, comes from a stumble. Absorbed by having gotten

---

39. Tolkien, J.R.R. *The Lord of the Rings*. Op. cit., p. 841.
40. Rank, O. *Double: A Psychoanalytic Study*. Op. cit., p. 76.
41. Rosset, C. *O Real e seu Duplo: Ensaio sobre a ilusão*. Op. cit., p. 83. The Latin in italic: 'the willing soul fate leads, but the unwilling drags along', in Richard Gummere's translation.

the Ring, Gollum falls into the abyss in a manner as stupid as his attachment to the Ring, a small but very dangerous object. "And [...] with a shriek he fell. Out of the depths came his last wail *Precious*, and he was gone."[42]

"This fantasy of being the other naturally ceases with death, because it is I who dies and not my double".[43] Sméagol/ Gollum's death is the only way through which he can be freed from the tyranny of the double, but maybe not from the anguish of his (non) existence.

This is probably the most fascinating thing about this character: there is not one closed answer about him. Because he brings this very evident dichotomy, we feel repulsion, but also empathy, maybe even compassion. His instability conveys what is unexpected in every individual, the everyday fight between our most noble and most vile desires.

Few are the fictional characters that display such an inner life. About that, Tolkien says in one of his letters:

"Gollum is to me just a 'character' – an imagined person – who granted the situation acted so and so under opposing strains, as it appears to be *probable* that he would (there is always an incalculable element in any individual real or imagined: otherwise he/she would not be an individual but a 'type')".[44]

The look upon the other

Gollum's relationship with other people could not be different from the one he had with himself and his double. We will observe especially the trio Frodo, Sam, and Gollum to provide a more specific analysis of his friendly relationships.

In *The Two Towers*, Sam and Frodo discover that Gollum was following them and, as soon as they find him, before he could notice, Sam tries to get hold of him, but he needed

42. Tolkien, J.R.R. *The Lord of the Rings*. Op. cit., p. 1238.
43. Rosset, C. *O Real e seu Duplo: Ensaio sobre a ilusão*. Op. cit., p. 86.
44. Tolkien, J.R.R., Carpenter, H. (Org.), Tolkien, C. (Assist.). *The Letters of J.R.R. Tolkien*. London: HarperCollins, 2006, Letter 181, p. 233.

Frodo's help with Sting, *The Hobbit*'s sword. "Things would have gone ill with Sam, if he had been alone".[45] From that moment on, *The Hobbits* discuss what they should do with that stalker creature, and Frodo remembers Gandalf's words when they still were in the Shire: it was Pity and Mercy, not wrath that determined Bilbo's decisions before Gollum.

That is how Frodo, as Bilbo had done, gave Gollum a chance. As the Ring-bearer, Baggins knew the effect the object had upon him and so he could feel pity and mercy towards that miserable creature. This passage of the book agrees with Thomas Aquinas saying: "a defect is always the reason for taking pity, either because one looks upon another's defect as one's own, through being united to him by love, or on account of the possibility of suffering in the same way".[46] The theologian goes on to define "mercy": "mercy takes its name "misericordia" from denoting a man's compassionate heart [*miserum cor*] for another's unhappiness".[47]

That does not mean that, between them, there is a seal of friendship. Aristotle claims that some people think "that a good man is the same as a friend"[48] and that, for friendship to happen, "must wish each other's good [...] and be aware of each other's feelings.".[49] If such reciprocity of wishing well to the other is absent, what is left is only goodwill.

Moreover, as we have seen in the first chapter, the classical text brings three types of friendship, two incidental ones, that may spring out of utility or pleasure, and a perfect type, which happens when both friends wish well mutually. Frodo shows benevolence towards Gollum. More than that, he is merciful. His goodness reaches beyond the creature's death, because, after he falls into the chasm of Mount Doom, Frodo forgives him, acknowledging that, without Gollum's help, the Ring

---

45. Tolkien, J.R.R. *The Lord of the Rings*. Op. cit., p. 802.
46. Aquinas, T. *The Summa Theologica*. Translated by the Fathers of the English Dominican province. London: Catholic Way Publishing, 2014,. SS Q30, A2.
47. Id., SS Q30, A1.
48. Aristotle. *The Nicomachean Ethics*. Op. cit., p. 252.
49. Id., p. 255.

would not be destroyed. But *The Hobbit* also had his debt with the former Ring-bearer: "One good turn deserves another".[50] By saying that, Frodo expected Gollum to lead the way to Mordor, where the Ring would be destroyed.

This means that the relationship between Frodo (and Sam) and Gollum is based on mutual interest, because Gollum only follows Frodo because he is incapable of keeping his distance from the Ring, while Gamgee and Baggins need to find their way to Mordor. But, before that, Frodo makes Gollum promise he will not attack him, removing the rope that they had tied around his *ankle*.

Peter Jackson's movie, it is interesting to note, opted for a more impactful effect by tying the rope around Gollum's *neck*, not his *ankle*. However, in the chapter "The Council of Elrond", Aragorn relates how he had captured Gollum near the Dead Marshes and handed him to the Elves — then the miserable creature told Gandalf everything that had happened since he found the Ring. On that occasion, Aragorn had tied the rope around Gollum's *neck*: "I deemed it the worst part of all my journey [...] making him walk before me with a halter on his neck, gagged".[51] The fact that Frodo chose to tie him by the ankle and not the neck is already a hint of his merciful and compassionate attitude to the creature, while Aragorn's heart was colder before Gollum. The movie does not make that distinction.

Freed from the rope, Gollum promises not to harm them by the Precious, the only thing that interests him. However, his attachment to the Ring is not a choice anymore due to the strong effect caused by Sauron's artefact. Therefore, one cannot say that he feels any liking even for the Precious. Gollum calls Frodo his "master" only because he is the Ring-bearer. In the following quotation, Frodo's lines give away some of what will happen on the outcome of the plot:

---

50. Tolkien, J.R.R. *The Lord of the Rings*. Op. cit., p. 804.
51. Id., p. 330.

> You swore a promise by what you call the Precious. Remember
> that! It will hold you to it; but it will seek a way to twist it to your
> own undoing. [...] If I, wearing it, were to command you, you would
> obey, even if it were *to leap from a precipice or to cast yourself into
> the fire*. And such would be my command.[52]

In *Homo Ludens*, Johan Huizinga calls the attention to the etymology of the words *prize*, *praise* and *price* (and, why not, *precious*?), from Latin *pretium*, which would have appeared in a context of exchange and valuation, presupposing something valuable. If we consider the relationship between the three wayfarers, the Ring is, for Gollum, a prize. Frodo and Sam's intention is simply to destroy it: Baggins keeps to his mission of bearer and destroyer of the evil object, and Sam is his loyal friend in this journey. But Gollum and Bilbo's heir compete for the Ring — at first, only until they reach Mordor — and both love and hate the object made by Sauron.

The interests of this trio are complex. Sam, Frodo's gardener, cannot stand Gollum or Sméagol, Stinker and Slinker as he calls the two sides of his personalities. Sam's mission of protecting Frodo is shaken by Gollum's presence. Baggins feels compassion towards Gollum, because only those who have born the Ring know how heavy a burden it is and, at the same time, he needs him to reach his destination. Lastly, Gollum is under an obligation with his master *because* of the Ring the master holds.

He cannot steal Frodo's Ring because the promise he made by the object prevents him from doing so. But why would such a powerful object allow such a promise to be made before it, seeing that Frodo wanted to destroy it? In a subtle way, the text suggests that there are other forces acting to destroy the One Ring.

Still in Hobbiton, where Frodo lived, Gandalf reveals some facts to him: "Bilbo was *meant* to find the Ring, and *not* by its

---

52. Id., pp. 836-837.

maker. In which case you also were *meant* to have it".[53] The author does not make it clear who was acting in the designs of Sauron's object, but he suggests that a being superior to Sauron himself guided the Ring's destiny, probably aiming at its destruction, since this being (or beings) was not or were not in favour of the Dark Lord.

A memorable characteristic we find in Gollum is his constant self-pity: "Poor, poor Sméagol, he went away long ago. They took his Precious, and he's lost now".[54] Also, he has a very childish behaviour, almost as that of an abandoned pet.

The lack of self-confidence makes Gollum suspicious of his companions, which eventually leads invariably to wickedness, as stated in the book's prologue: "after ages alone in the dark Gollum's heart was black, and treachery was in it".[55] Frodo is the exact opposite. *The Hobbit* is humble and honest with himself and the others; acquiescent of his mission, he does not complain to himself or the world, and accepts his destiny.

When Gollum is taken and questioned by Faramir, secondborn of the steward of Gondor, because he had trespassed and entered the forbidden pool in Henneth Annûn, Frodo calls upon Gollum's trust: "I'll go with you, and you shall come to no harm. Not unless they kill me too. Trust Master!", to which Gollum, always suspicious, "turned and spat at him".[56]

Frodo was true to his word; "But I promised that if he came to me, he should not be harmed. And I would not be proved faithless."[57] On the other hand, Gollum starts to pretend he trusts Master but, from then on, and more than ever, he commits to his plan of leading him to the giant spider Shelob.

Sam, in turn, is an obstacle to Gollum, who had no interest in letting Gamgee live. However, the promise he made to Frodo also extended to the gardener. Thus, not only does Sam

---

53. Tolkien, J.R.R. *The Lord of the Rings*. Op. cit., p. 73.
54. Id., p. 805.
55. Id., p. 16.
56. Id., p. 900.
57. Id., p. 902.

protect Frodo, but also the opposite.

A remarkable passage in the book is when Sam asks Gollum to fetch them food, and he brings two small rabbits, which he wants to eat right away, raw. Sam, evidently appalled, cooks them with herbs, to Gollum's disgust. This scene shows the distance and absence of bonds between them: "Sharing meals is one of the things that most unites men".[58]

Sam and Frodo share their meal, but Gollum does not take part in that. Sam says: "Our bread chokes you, and raw coney chokes me".[59] Gollum had, then, to find his own food (raw fish) alone.

All these attitudes and circumstances considered, it seems evident that there is no friendship between Gollum and *The Hobbit*s. While there are interests, there is no pleasure in being together. Above all, there is no mutual benevolence. Friendship and companionship give way to competition and dissimulation (mostly on Gollum's side).

Angles and Reverse Angles: Points of view in dialogue

It is worth taking a closer look to the portrayal of Gollum in the cinematographic trilogy *The Lord of the Rings*, particularly *The Two Towers* (2002) and *The Return of the King* (2003). The intention is to understand better the choices made by the production team to represent this complex character in a new language, having in mind the Self, the Double, and their relationship.

Resuming Aristotle's claim that the friend is "his second self",[60] we will now focus on Gollum's internal dialogues in the above-mentioned movies to approach the representation of the Self, the Double, and how both independent personalities interact in the same character, Sméagol/Gollum.

58. Martins Filho, I. G. *Ética e Ficção de Aristóteles a Tolkien*. São Paulo: Elsevier, 2010, p. 220.
59. Tolkien, J.R.R. *The Lord of the Rings*. Op. cit., p. 855.
60. Aristotle. *The Nicomachean Ethics*. Op. cit., p. 295.

According to Marcel Martin, while dialogues are not a specific element of the cinema (such as the montage, for instance), they deserve close attention, since words also constitute the projected image. Elements such as soundtrack, sound design, setting, and light design are also very important to convey ideas and sensations to the spectator, not to mention the performance of the actor in his or her role. For Martin, *"every reality, event or gesture is a symbol – or, more precisely, a sign – in some degree"*, adding that *"the significance of an image depends much on the interplay with neighbouring images"*.[61]

Gollum's internal dialogues happen in dark, gloomy settings, or in sinuous paths, full of rocks, ups and downs, in mysterious or disturbing environments, and their dynamics follow the character's movement, along with the light and the setting where he is.

The internal conflict displayed in the dialogue is often highlighted by the close-ups and the montage with the interplay between different kinds of shot.[62] For Martin,

> "[the purpose] of most shots is the convenience of perception and the clarity of the narrative. Only the *extreme close-up* (and the *big close-up* which, from the psychological point of view, practically intermingles with it) and the *long shot*[63] have, most of the times, a precise psychological significance and not only a descriptive role".[64]

As for the close-ups, very much used for Gollum and Sméagol's internal dialogue, it is worthwhile to recall Martin's

---

61. Martin, M. *A Linguagem Cinematográfica*. São Paulo: Brasiliense, 2011, p. 92. Emphasis by the author.
62. As we have seen, the shot refers to the distance between the camera and the object. The medium shots (MS) include the person from waist up; the close-ups (CU) show the person's head and shoulders, but can also show only the face of a character (a "big close-up", BCU) or even a detail of a character or object ("extreme close-up", ECU).
63. That is, the shot which includes the whole body or object.
64. Martin, M. *A Linguagem Cinematográfica*. Op. cit., pp. 37-38.

quote that cinema provides us with "intimacy because the image (again through the foreground) makes us literally penetrate the beings (by means of their faces, open books to the souls) and the things".[65] Corroborating our analysis, Otto Rank claims, concerning the "essential problem of the ego", that "the modern interpreter, who is supported or compelled by the new technique of representation, [prominently highlights] by using such a vivid language of imagery".[66]

The Double Characterization

It is impossible not to mention the physical description of the character. The movie evidently based its own description on Tolkien's, as shown in this passage:

> Down the face of a precipice, [...] a small black shape was moving with its thin limbs splayed out. Maybe its soft clinging hands and toes were finding crevices and holds that no hobbit could ever have seen or used, but it looked as if it was just creeping down on sticky pads, like some large prowling thing of insect-kind. And it was coming down head first, as if it was smelling its way. Now and again it lifted its head slowly, turning it right back on its long skinny neck, and *The Hobbit*s caught a glimpse of two small pale gleaming lights, its eyes that blinked at the moon for a moment and then were quickly lidded again.[67]

Based on this description, the art direction of the movie studied how it could be imprinted upon the character. The behind-the-scenes footage made by the team shows that Gollum's representation underwent several steps from the screenplay to the screen itself: drawings, sculptures, mock-ups, storyboards, animatics etc.

The artists who provided the basis for the whole art direction were the English Alan Lee and the Canadian John Howe, famous for their Tolkien-inspired illustrations. Both were the

65. Id., p. 25.
66. Rank, O. *The Double: A Psychoanalytic Study*. Op. cit., p. 7.
67. Tolkien, J.R.R. *The Lord of the Rings*. Op. cit., p. 800.

concept artists engaged in the production of *The Lord of the Rings* cinematographic trilogy.

At first, Gollum was intended to be produced solely by computer-graphic effects from Weta Workshop. But, after casting Andy Serkis to dub the character, everyone was impressed by the delivery of his performance, so that the whole team realised Gollum could not be made exclusively through computer graphics, even though this could not be eschewed altogether, since the physical performance of Gollum — his articulations, posture, and agility — was not compatible with that of a common person.

Serkis was then responsible for bringing much of the dramatic and expressive force to the character, and Weta Workshop was responsible for the technological part, without eschewing the character's performance, seeing that the digital artists frequently had to put themselves in the actor's position to design Gollum's expression in their computers.

Andy Serkis started to accompany the filming with the other actors with whom Gollum interacted. Besides that, he would also shoot in the studio so that, based on his acting, the digital team could build the finalised character by means of a technique called *motion capture*: markers are set on the actor's body, transmitting the character's movements to the computer — a modern version of the older method called *rotoscoping*. To that the producers added the animation technique, conferring more authenticity to the scenes, nicknaming it "roto-animation".

The result was an audiovisual construction at once human and bestial, compelling and repulsive — just as the character is supposed to be. The realistic computer graphics and Andy Serkis's engrossing performance brought to the cinematographic Gollum both truthfulness and empathy to the spectators.

Sméagol x Gollum

To analyse the internal dialogues as they are represented in the movies, let us first recall the book description:

Sméagol was holding a debate with some other thought that used the same voice but made it squeak and hiss. A pale light and a green light alternated in his eyes as he spoke.
'Sméagol promised,' said the first thought.
'Yes, yes, my precious,' came the answer, 'we promised: to save our Precious, not to let Him have it – never. […] if we was master, then we could help ourselfs, yes, and still keep promises.'
'But Sméagol said he would be very very good. […]'
'[…] Let's be good, good as fish, sweet one, but to ourselfs. […]'
'But the Precious holds the promise' […].
'Then take it,' said the other, 'and let's hold it ourselfs! Then we shall be master, gollum! Make the other hobbit, the nasty suspicious hobbit, make him crawl […]!'[68]

In the book, after this scene, the internal dialogues continue, but not as markedly. In the movies, this dialogue unfolds in four: three in *The Two Towers* — one of them very subtle, happening when Faramir captures Gollum — and one in *The Return of the King*. The corresponding scene in the movie, which the production team called "schizophrenia" — Gollum talking to himself, "Sméagol" — was so memorable in *The Two Towers* that they decided to explore the phenomenon of the double in *The Return of the King* too.

The resources used by the audiovisual producers to emphasise the difference in each one's eyes were the dilated pupils for Sméagol and constricted for Gollum, an appearance of naiveté and wickedness, respectively, as it is said in the above quotation: "A pale light and a green light alternated in his eyes as he spoke".

The internal dialogue scene, i.e., the "schizophrenia scene" as the team called it, was wholly assembled upon Andy Serkis's performance, something that did not always happen. It is a very dramatic scene and also hinged on the cinematographic language:

[Point of view shot: Gollum's gaze at Frodo's hand holding the ring while he sleeps (close-up; zoom in)]

68. Tolkien, J.R.R. *The Lord of the Rings*. Op. cit., pp. 827-828.

[Gollum's voice offscreen]
We wants it. We needs it.
[Cut to long shot. Dolly out[69] to the objective perspective]

[Gollum]
Must have the precious. They stole it from us. Sneaky little Hobbitses. Wicked. Tricksy. False.

[Tracking shot to the right]
[Sméagol (close-up)]
No. Not Master.

[Tracking shot to the left — Gollum]
Yes, precious. False. They will cheat you, hurt you, lie!

[Cut to the camera on the right, reverse angle — Sméagol]
Master's my friend.

[Cut to the camera on the left — Gollum]
You don't have any friends. Nobody likes you.

[Right — Sméagol (close-up)]
Not listening. I'm not listening.

[Left — Gollum]
You're a liar and a thief.

[Right — Sméagol at bay]
No.

[Left — Gollum, imposing, with constricted pupils]
Murderer. [Zoom in]

[Right — Sméagol at bay, whimpering]
Go away.

[Left — Gollum]
Go away?

[Right — Sméagol]
I hate you. I hate you.

---

69. The camera moves out without the interference of zooming.

[Left — Gollum]
Where would you be without me? [coughing] *Gollum. Gollum. I saved us. It was me. We survived because of me.*

[Right — Sméagol]
Not anymore.

[Left — Gollum]
What did you say?

[Right — Sméagol (close-up)]
Master looks after us now. We don't need you. [As though looking at Gollum]

[Left — Gollum (big close-up)]
What?

[Right — Sméagol (medium shot)]
Leave now and never come back. [Sméagol lowers his head]

[Cut to the right — Gollum raises his head (close-up)]
No.

[Right — Sméagol (close-up)]
Leave now and never come back.

[Left — Gollum growling (big close-up)]

[Right — Sméagol (medium shot)]
Leave now and never come back!

[Left — Sméagol alone (long shot)]

The setting is always shady, and the lighting is dark, suggesting Gollum's emotional condition: confused, mysterious, heavy. Sméagol is always looking down, except in the final moment, when he expels Gollum and looks as if he were in front of him. Sméagol's images are captured in longer shots than Gollum's. Close-ups and big close-ups become more frequent in Gollum as the dialogue develops, showing the psychological tension of the character and his position in front of his other self, Sméagol.

With the interplay of angle and reverse angle, Sméagol to the right and Gollum to the left, the montage expects the viewer to understand a message or concept. The spectators know that there are not two characters, but the internal dialogue is so intense that it splits the character expressively, so that we think that there are, indeed, two "selves" of a single creature — or none, for to be many is to be no one. In this case,

The closing-up of shots is not based upon a material relationship, directly or scientifically explicable: the connections are made in the spectators' minds and, in its limit, may be refused by them; it is up to the director to be sufficiently persuasive.[70]

We also note that, at first, the camera is tracking, and only after that does the interplay between angle/reverse angle start: Sméagol to the right and Gollum to the left. This helps the spectator realise that it is one single character in the same scene, not a memory, or imagination, or another scene. An interesting resource was showing that Gollum "left" at the end by showing Sméagol alone, this time in a long shot from the left, which had been Gollum's position: we, the spectators, understand this interplay because of the rhythm of the montage combined with the dialogue.

All these techniques facilitate the understanding that at stake is an internal dialogue that slowly gains momentum, reaching, at the apex, the appearance of a game that sometimes resembles a case of schizophrenia and sometimes seems to be on the verge of the fantastic universe. If we use Todorov's analysis of fantastic literature[71] (which we can extend to other artistic categories, such as Cinema, as suggested by David Roas),[72] the concept of "fantastic" lies in the tension and doubt between concrete reality ("Primary World", in Tolkienian terms), and the fantastic world ("Secondary World"). The "uncanny" event, in turn, would be scientifically explainable.

70. Martin, M. *A Linguagem Cinematográfica*. Op. cit., p. 153.
71. Todorov, T. *Introdução à Literatura Fantástica*. São Paulo: Perspectiva, 2004.
72. Roas, D. *A Ameaça do Fantástico*. São Paulo: Editora Unesp, 2014.

By calling the scene "schizophrenia", the team remove the possibility of a "fantastic" meaning using psychiatry nomenclature, that is, something explained by science, leaving Gollum's double in the realm of the "uncanny" genre. But if we remember that Tolkien's writings are hinged on the "marvellous" element, through which all the mythic phenomena are accepted in the story without question, and that Gollum's internal tension is provoked not only by his personal behaviour, but mainly through the Ring's action, we can come up with the hypothesis that Gollum is an uncanny element within a marvellous universe.[73]

However, this also leaves us in a dubious and hesitant position as to what really happens with Gollum/Sméagol, something quite relatable to what Todorov calls "fantastic". This happens also in the movies: even though the producers called it "schizophrenia", one cannot say that Gollum was merely a creature with psychological issues, but one cannot say that his double personality is solely a product of magical actions either. It is a combination of these phenomena. It is possible, then, to affirm that Gollum is a fantastic element within a high-fantasy work, one whose universe is meticulously explained to convince the reader that there is coherence in every detail of that literary Subcreation.

Going back to the internal dialogue of the character in the movie, we notice that, at the end, Sméagol sends Gollum away, but this does not happen in the book. The screenplay shows Sméagol's trust in Frodo, at first, which is later lost. This helps the spectator feel empathy and compassion, identifying with him and sharing his suffering. Thus, the spectator is at once confused by and connected with him when the character chooses to take revenge on Frodo.

There is also a further interesting book/movie difference in the relationship between Baggins and Gollum: in the book, but not in the movie, Frodo is aware of Gollum's bad intentions

---

73. *The Lord of the Rings* is regarded as "fantasy", in which marvellous tales are conjoined with the making of myths by the author's Subcreation (mythopoeia).

from the beginning. In the audiovisual production, Frodo is apparently naïve at the beginning, while Sam knows better. The literary narrative certainly wanted to show that, by being aware of Gollum's weaknesses, his mercy towards the vile creature would grow stronger. In the movie, the option for building rapport between the spectators and Gollum facilitates the acceptance of Frodo's benevolence towards him. In this latter case, Frodo's mercy loses some of its power.

The screenwriters' decision shows the need for Sméagol to shun his double, who disturbs and enslaves him. "The refusal of the unity is, incidentally, only one of the more general forms of the refusal of life. That is why the elimination of the double announces, on the contrary, the vigorous return of the real, comparable to the joy of a completely new morning".[74]

The last scene in *The Two Towers* resumes Gollum and Sméagol's internal dialogue, in which the plan to hand Frodo to Shelob is made explicit. The double comes with full strength, and the movie ends under the tension of what is to come:

[Tracking shot following Sméagol walking in the woods — crawling (long shot)]

Master. Master looks after us.
Master
wouldn't hurt us.
Master broke his promise.

[...]

[Close-up]

We could let her do it.
Yes. She could do it.
Yes, precious, she could. And then we takes it once they're dead.
Once they're dead.
Shhh...

---

74. Rosset, C. *O Real e seu Duplo: Ensaio sobre a ilusão*. Op. cit., pp. 82-83.

In this scene, there is no distinction between angle and reverse angle shots for us to know there are two personalities in a single being. This had already been shown in the "schizophrenia" scene. Gollum walks fast with his thoughts, and the camera follows him, as though he were dodging *The Hobbits*. The camera stops, and the shot gets closer in moments of greater emphasis in the psychological tension.

In *The Return of the King*, there is a further scene that highlights internal dialogue. As it is an independent movie, even though part of a cohesive trilogy, the scene also serves the purpose of resuming the ideas in *The Two Towers* and emphasising the devilish plan of a confused Gollum. This time, the montage opts for a parallelism that reaches the sphere of metaphor: Sméagol talks to his image, Gollum, reflected on a pool:

The scene unfolds thus:

[Sméagol is having a nightmare. He gets up, goes to a pool, where he sees his own reflection (Gollum)]

[Sméagol has his back to the camera and talks to the reflection — Gollum (big close-up)]
What is it saying, my Precious, my love? Is Sméagol losing his nerve?

[Sméagol, outside the pool (close-up)]
No! Not! Never!! Sméagol hates nasty Hobbitses! Sméagol wants to see them dead!

[Gollum's reflection (big close-up)]
And we will. Sméagol did it once. He can do it again.

[Flash scene of Sméagol strangling Déagol][75]

[The creature appears on the camera to the left (Sméagol, outside the lake, turns into the same Gollum of the reflection)]
It's ours! Ours!

---

75. While in the book this scene occurs in *The Fellowship of the Ring*, it is depicted in the last movie, *The Return of the King*, on the first scene.

[Sméagol comes to himself, and his pupils dilate once again]
We must get the Precious. We must get it back!

[...]

[Gollum's reflection (big close-up)]
[...] *then we will find it!*

[Sméagol (medium shot)]
And take it for me!

[Gollum's reflection (big close-up)]
For us.

[Sméagol (medium shot)]
Yes, we, we meant "for us".

[Reverse angle shot showing Sméagol, with his back to the camera, looking at his reflection (Gollum), as in the beginning, suggesting that there is only one creature]
Gollum. Gollum. [Coughing] *The Precious will be ours* [big close-up] *once The Hobbitses are dead!*

By seeing his reflection (Gollum) on the water, Sméagol symbolises himself before a mirror, an object commonly present in representations of the double, and also refers us more clearly to the myth of Narcissus, who met his sad fate reflected upon the waters. The visual language conveys the message of the character's search for his own self. Without words, only with images, the movie presents the anguish of the "self" in each of us, who never know ourselves completely. In that regard, Clément Rosset claims:

I know well the unicity of everything that surrounds me [...] This does not happen with my 'self', which I have never seen nor will ever see, not even in a mirror. Because the mirror is deceitful and constitutes 'false evidence', that is, the illusion of a vision, it shows me not my 'self', but a reverse, someone else.[76]

---

76. Rosset, C. *O Real e seu Duplo: Ensaio sobre a ilusão.* Op. cit., p. 79.

Again, the montage gives the spectator the task of interpreting the scene, showing what the character wants to see in the reflection of the pool, "that thing towards which it turns mentally",[77] and also what the mythical force of the Ring makes him see. By means of such richness, complexity, and competence of the producers, the movie can boast of a high-quality status in scenes such as these ones with an internal dialogue. For Martin:

> [...] there are movies [...] which reveal a curious subversion of values and a patent ignorance of the realistic nature of cinema. Such movies transform the directly legible appearance of the action (the first degree of a movie's intelligibility) into a simple support, artificially contrived to imply a symbolic meaning (the second degree of intelligibility), which takes on a position of high importance. Such movies break the "rules of the cinematographic game", which intends the image to be, first, a piece of directly significant reality and, after that, accessorily and optionally, the mediator of a more profound and general signification.[78]

It is true that the character, born in literature, helped the movie gain a more symbolic status, but it is undeniable that the moviemakers did this very competently. By means of dialogue, settings, symbols, lighting, and other elements not analysed here (such as soundtrack, sound design, and costume design), Peter Jackson and his team tried to capture the essence of Tolkien's character, including his internal crisis in search of the self, the conflict with his double and his relationship with the others.

In the analysis of friendship, both in the book and the movie, Sméagol/Gollum bears an important interior conflict, showing that the relationship with himself reflects the one with the others. Sméagol loses his identity to Gollum: by turning inwards, he ends up being no one. He loves and hates himself, as he does with the others and the Ring itself. Very much

77. Martin, M. *A Linguagem Cinematográfica*. Op. cit., p. 138.
78. Id., pp. 105-106.

linked to the magical object, a symbol of the Universal Self, Gollum gradually loses his shape, living long years in endless affliction, having barely a choice other than death.

Without unity in life, Sméagol-Gollum finds no occasion to love himself or other people whom he could call friends. Gollum's behaviour in the book is stronger than in the movie (in which he tries, at first, to gain the spectators' empathy by being more comical or pleasant), but it still wavers, arousing compassion in the reader as well.

Gollum symbolises our weaknesses, our wicked disposition, and the attachment to one's self. He is also the object of our hatred, because he shows the sad fate that awaits us if we do not forget a little our own selves and be open to the other, because friendship is "most necessary to our life".[79] In this sense, a character that could be set in contrast with Gollum is Sam, because he chose different paths. In the next chapter, we will focus on him and other close friends of Frodo's.

	Books	**Movies**
Sméagol's versus Gollum's eyes	Alternating pale and green light.	Dilated/constricted pupils.
Internal dialogues	One significant in *The Two Towers*	Three significant ones in *The Two Towers*, and one in *The Return of the King*.
Frodo's behaviour	Merciful: aware of Gollum's wickedness.	More naïve in relation to Gollum. His mercy is weaker in comparison to the book.
Gollum's behaviour	Gollum's dark, selfish, and vain side is evident and preponderant from the beginning.	Slightly more comical to gain the spectators' empathy. The selfish and treacherous sides grow gradually.

79. Aristotle. *The Nicomachean Ethics*. Op. cit., p. 251.

Chapter Four

United by the same ideal

When Gandalf told Frodo about the origins and the power of the Ring, *The Hobbit* soon volunteered to leave the Shire,[1] to Gandalf's surprise:

> 'My dear Frodo!' exclaimed Gandalf. 'Hobbits really are amazing creatures, as I have said before. You can learn all that there is to know about their ways in a month, and yet after a hundred years they can still surprise you at a pinch.'[2]

Gandalf's statement shows how interesting *The Hobbit*s are, even though they are unknown or despised by the majority of the peoples in Middle-earth. Moreover, by saying "not even from you", Gandalf shows that, among *The Hobbit*s, who already are special creatures, Frodo Baggins, Bilbo's heir, stands out for his personal values.

The Hobbit would have left the Shire alone were it not for the fact that his gardener, Samwise Gamgee, had overheard great part of the conversation. As a consequence of his curiosity, Gamgee was invited to depart with his master, which was a great joy to him, after all the stories of the world beyond the Shire fascinated him and, besides, Sam did not want to leave Mr. Frodo.

Baggins tried to leave the Shire discreetly, pretending to be moving to another dwelling. Following Gandalf's advice,

---

1. In the movie, one has the impression that Frodo left as soon as Gandalf explained everything to him. But the book makes it clear that five months elapsed after Frodo's decision. Besides, the conversation they have about the Ring happened almost ten years after Bilbo's party. The literary text is also clear in showing that Frodo's decision, however prompt, was also a difficult one.

2. Tolkien, J.R.R. *The Lord of the Rings*. London: HarperCollins, 2008, p. 82.

he decided to go towards the elven town of Rivendell, where Bilbo was to be found. His plan was to part with his best friends, Meriadoc Brandybuck (Merry) and Peregrin Took (Pippin), during the apparent move, and then follow to Rivendell with Sam, where he intended to meet Gandalf, who had not sent any news yet.

However, his friends had already discovered Frodo's plans, with Sam's help, because they had for a long time been observing Bilbo and his nephew. When Merry and Pippin revealed their discovery to Frodo, they give a great lesson on friendship. In Merry's words:

> 'You can trust us to stick to you through thick and thin – to the bitter end. And you can trust us to keep any secret of yours – closer than you keep it yourself. But you cannot trust us to let you face trouble alone, and go off without a word. We are your friends, Frodo.'[3]

With this, Merry and Pippin show to Frodo three indispensable elements for friendship: interest (meaning 'to care about the other'), trust, and faithfulness. We can say that these elements are contained in what Aristotle calls "benevolence", that is, wishing well to the other. Whoever wishes well to their friend is interested in that which is important for their companion, is attentive to the details concerning the other, because what interests a friend is their interest too. What would look like the mere curiosity of two naughty Hobbits is, in fact, an expression of love. If, to his friends' eyes, Frodo had been behaving strangely, they did not misinterpret it, and trusted him: "You can trust us to stick to you through thick and thin – to the bitter end". Also, there is the issue of faithfulness: they will follow him "like hounds", no matter what happens.

Such attitudes require reciprocity: they are his friends because they know Frodo would do the same for them and, thus, Bilbo's heir agrees to proceed in Merry, Pippin, and Sam's company. Frodo goes with them to Rivendell to learn

---

3. Tolkien, J.R.R. *The Lord of the Rings*. Op. cit., p. 138.

more about what should be done with the Ring, not without going through a number of adventures and misfortunes. The truth is that, without his three companions, and other friends he found along the way, Frodo would not have gotten there, and this was only the beginning.

One threat, multiple heroes

At the end of the first volume of the saga, *The Fellowship of the Ring*, the reader witnesses the breaking of the fellowship — constituted of two Men, Aragorn and Boromir; four Hobbits, Frodo, Sam, Merry, and Pippin; the Wizard Gandalf; the Dwarf Gimli; and the Elf Legolas. From that moment on, Frodo and Sam follow on their own to Mordor, where the Ring must be destroyed, and the other members of the fellowship take distinct paths.

According to Maria Nikolajeva, an expert in comparative literature, *The Lord of the Rings* would be considered an adult novel, not a children's book, unlike *The Hobbit*, because it displays parallel plots as from the breaking of *The Fellowship of the Ring*. She argues:

> Auxiliary and parallel plots allow the reader to follow several characters one at a time. It may be necessary and desirable for the actions involved; however, it limits the scope of characterization. While an adult novel of 800 pages can have a number of parallel plots and yet leave ample room for the portrayal of several characters, a children's novel of 120 pages does not have the same prerequisites.[4]

This may be the main reason why *The Lord of the Rings* has over a thousand pages, not counting appendices and maps. Space was needed to develop the actions of the plot and the characterization and development of characters. Tolkien talks about that, displaying his peculiar humour:

---

4. Nikolajeva, M. *The Rhetoric of Character in Children's Literature*. Lanham, Maryland: The Scarecrow Press, 2003, p. 162.

The prime motive [to tell the story] was the desire of a tale-teller to try his hand at a really long story that would hold the attention of readers, amuse them, delight them, and at times maybe excite them or deeply move them. [...] Some who have read the book, or at any rate have reviewed it, have found it boring, absurd, or contemptible; and I have no cause to complain, since I have similar opinions of their works, or of the kinds of writing that they evidently prefer. [...] The most critical reader of all, myself, now finds many defects, minor and major, but being fortunately under no obligation either to review the book or to write it again, he will pass over these in silence, except one that has been noted by others: the book is too short.[5]

The circumstance that caused the breaking of *The Fellowship of the Ring* was the fact that one of its members, Boromir, firstborn of Gondor Steward, decided to take the Ring from Frodo when *The Hobbit*, in a moment of seclusion, was making up his mind about where they should go from there. If Merry and Pippin were an example of how to help a friend in distress, Boromir was an example of what *not* to do in that case. First, he insists he is a true man, even though he acts with little honesty, dominated by his passions, using little reason. Boromir prefers to win through strength instead of pondering what the best way is to destroy the object that threatens the peoples of Middle-earth. Just like Sauron — and, therefore, the Ring itself — the son of Denethor, at that moment, believes that strength gives him power and freedom. On the other hand, Frodo's wisdom, who does not want power for himself, makes him "worthy" of being the Ring-bearer. Even if, at the end, he surrenders a little to power, being unable to throw the Ring in the fire, he is humble enough to be the one who got closer to doing that among all the characters in the story.

It is worth remembering that, in *The Nicomachean Ethics*, Aristotle studies the chief good of Men, friendship being a part of it, and virtue being a condition for the sought-for happiness.

---

5. Tolkien, J.R.R. *The Lord of the Rings*. Op. cit., pp. xxvi-xxvii.

The philosopher reminds, also, about the importance of a virtuous man using reason:

> The function of man, then, is exercise of his vital faculties [or soul] on one side in obedience to reason, and on the other side with reason. [...] (Man's function then being, as we say, a kind of life — that is to say, exercise of his faculties and action of various kinds with reason — the good man's function is to do this well and beautifully [or nobly]. But the function of anything is done well when it is done in accordance with the proper excellence of that thing.) If this be so the result is that the good of man is exercise of his faculties in accordance with excellence or virtue, or, if there be more than one, in accordance with the best and most complete virtue [...].[6]

Boromir is not reasonable when he is close to the Ring, which culminates in his violent attitude towards Frodo, precisely when *The Hobbit* was secluded, thinking about his further steps. As is typical for the power of the Ring, it brings forward and emphasises the vile side of people: it revealed Boromir's darkest side. The captain of Gondor wanted to solve, first and foremost, his own problems, with no regard to the group decision; he wanted to go to Minas Tirith and see his people, without having in mind the profit of every people in Middle-earth involved in the war against Sauron's power. What the captain of Gondor did not know was that, by thinking this way, he would also bring suffering to his own people. He did not display enough longanimity or meekness to solve the imminent problem.

Sam, Merry, and Pippin made ready to follow their friend in a faithful way, based on trust. Boromir, in turn, started showing one of the main characteristics of the malign power of the Ring: betrayal. Evil in *The Lord of the Rings* is normally characterised by disloyalty among fellows.

One of the best examples to illustrate this is when Saruman,

---

6. Aristotle. *The Nicomachean Ethics*, trans. by F. H. Peters, 10 edn. London: Kegan Paul, Trench, Trübner & Co., 1906, pp. 16-17.

Gandalf's leader, decides to take the Ring for himself instead of joining forces with his Wizard fellow in the war *against* the Ring — as a consequence, Saruman is himself betrayed, and murdered by Gríma Wormtongue, his servant, when he tries to take over the Shire after the fall of the Ring. As Aristotle points out:

> But people who are not good cannot be of one mind, just as they cannot be friends except for a little space or to a slight extent, as they strive for more than their share of profit, but take less than their share of labours and public services [...].[7]

Ironically, Boromir accuses Frodo of disloyalty: "Miserable trickster! [...] You will take the Ring to Sauron and sell us all. You have only waited your chance to leave us in the lurch".[8] However, Boromir is not wholly taken by evil and has a redemptive death. After trying to take the Ring from Frodo and coming to himself, he finds the other companions of the Fellowship and fights off a number of Uruk-hai orcs, who, by order of Saruman, had the mission of capturing *The Hobbit*s they found. The Gondorian, defending Merry and Pippin, ends up wounded by arrows and is found by Aragorn moments before his death. Just like one who confesses before a priest, Boromir bids farewell to life with the blessings of the future King of his people:

> Aragorn knelt beside him. Boromir opened his eyes and strove to speak. At last slow words came. 'I tried to take the Ring from Frodo,' he said. 'I am sorry. I have paid. [...]
> 'No!' said Aragorn, taking his hand and kissing his brow. 'You have conquered. Few have gained such a victory. Be at peace! Minas Tirith shall not fall!'[9]

The son of Gondor Steward is not the first one to be severed from the Fellowship. Before that, in Moria, they suffered their

---

7. Aristotle. *The Nicomachean Ethics.* Op. cit., p. 300.
8. Tolkien, J.R.R. *The Lord of the Rings.* Op. cit., pp. 520-521.
9. Id., p. 538.

first great loss: Gandalf, then the leader of the Fellowship, fell into the abyss with the Balrog, a Demon of Morgoth. Gandalf the Grey left the Fellowship and, forlorn, they moved on with Aragorn as their leader. Later, the wizard reappeared to his friends Aragorn, Legolas, and Gimli as "Gandalf the White" in Fangorn Forest.

As a Maia, Gandalf does not originally have a mortal, physical shape, which was granted to him when he voyaged to Middle-earth in aid of its inhabitants. By falling into the abyss and fighting the Balrog, he suffered and left Middle-earth. But he resumes his mission with a new condition: he is not the Grey any longer, but the White, as Saruman had been before. In a letter, Tolkien explains this important part of the mythology:

> Gandalf really 'died', and was changed [...] I [would] venture to say that he was an incarnate 'angel'– strictly an ἄγγελος: that is, with the other Istari, wizards, 'those who know', an emissary from the Lords of the West, sent to Middle-earth, as the great crisis of Sauron loomed on the horizon. [...] The 'wizards' were not exempt, indeed being incarnate were more likely to stray, or err. Gandalf alone fully passes the tests, on a moral plane anyway (he makes mistakes of judgement). For in his condition it was for him a sacrifice to perish on the Bridge in defence of his companions. [...] He was sent by a mere prudent plan of the angelic Valar or governors; but Authority had taken up this plan and enlarged it, at the moment of its failure [...]; for he passed 'out of thought and time' [...], 'unclothed like a child' (not discarnate), and so ready to receive the white robes of the highest.[10]

When Gandalf departs, the companions feel as orphans, and even though Aragorn has the profile of a leader, he lacks the wizard's wisdom, knowledge, and power. Besides, Gandalf either represents, or indeed is, the spiritual presence of the Fellowship, and parting with him resembles those moments in life in which we, even the ones who believe in a deity, feel lonely and forsaken, although only apparently.

---

10. Tolkien, J.R.R., Carpenter, H. (Org.), Tolkien, C. (Assist.). *The Letters of J.R.R. Tolkien*. London: HarperCollins, 2006, Letter 156, pp. 201-203.

The absence of the Istar left more room for Boromir to act violently against Frodo and the Ring. After his duel with the Gondorian, Frodo decided he must go along, because the Ring started acting more strongly in the Fellowship, causing divisions and trying to prevent the Quest from being successful.

Frodo's decision cost him a great deal of effort, as it had happened before when he left the Shire bearing Isildur's Bane, and even more when he volunteered in the Council of Elrond to bear the Ring to Mordor. But such decisions were crucial for his growth, enabling him to gradually overcome his denial of his mission and move on.

The decision of going alone brought doubt, fear, and... temptation. To escape from Boromir, Frodo put the Ring on and, suddenly, the magical object started acting on him. From the top of the hill of Amon Hen, on the Seat of Seeing, he had a glimpse of the Dark Lord's action over Middle-earth: "everywhere he looked he saw the signs of war".[11] After this external view, something even more intense started working inside him:

> And suddenly he felt the Eye. [...] A fierce eager will was there. It leaped towards him; almost like a finger he felt it, searching for him. [...]
> He heard himself crying out: *Never, never!* Or was it: *Verily I come, I come to you?* He could not tell. [...] Then as a flash from some other point of power there came to his mind another thought: *Take it off! Take it off! Fool, take it off! Take off the Ring!*
> The two powers strove in him. For a moment, perfectly balanced between their piercing points, he writhed, tormented.[12]

The forces acting inside Frodo's head, the Eye and the Voice, were Sauron and Gandalf respectively. That is something we realise much later, when Gandalf, already the White, tells his friends, Aragorn, Gimli, and Legolas, that he had received some news about Frodo:

---

11. Tolkien, J.R.R. *The Lord of the Rings*. Op. cit., p. 522.
12. Id., p. 523.

'[...] The Ring now has passed beyond my help, or the help of any of the Company that set out from Rivendell. Very nearly it was revealed to the Enemy, but it escaped. I had some part in that: for I sat in a high place, and I strove with the Dark Tower; and the Shadow passed [...]'[13]

Frodo had to find himself free of the Eye and the Voice for one moment to make a decision on his own. The choice of proceeding alone to the Enemy's land almost worked out, were it not for an essential element: Sam once again notices the absence and finds him before he could cross the river on his way to Mordor; and he does not allow Frodo to go alone. Sam and his master, then, went to the East together, leaving the rest of the Fellowship behind.

Such a branching of plots, generated by the breaking (physical, not ideological) of *The Fellowship of the Ring* enabled some previously minor characters to develop and gain a heroic status. Besides that, the split of the fellowship opened room for their friendship to grow, thus helping the fulfilment of their collective objective, despite the differences the members had.

The comparatist Maria Nikolajeva emphasises that it is not so simple to find the protagonists who, according to her, are at the centre of the plot, around whom the story revolves. She offers some criteria to detect who the protagonist is. The first is the appearance of the character's name in the title. *The Lord of the Rings* refers to the main antagonist of the story, because it is Sauron who forges the One Ring, which rules all the other rings. However, we cannot say that he is the main character of the story, but the one who brings the problem around which the plot revolves, as is typical for antagonists.

The order of appearance would be another criterion to define the protagonist. In this case, Tolkien gives us hints of the main role played by the Hobbits, since his story starts in the Shire, when Bilbo is preparing a party for his "eleventy-first" birthday in the chapter "A Long-expected Party". But a hasty

---

13. Id., p. 646.

reader could jump to the conclusion that the story, a sequel to *The Hobbit*, has Bilbo as its central character again, and that impression stretches up to the Council of Elrond, in Rivendell, when there is still a possibility of Bilbo becoming once again the Ring-bearer: 'Very well, very well, Master Elrond!' […] Bilbo the silly hobbit started this affair, and Bilbo had better finish it, or himself...'[14]

Gandalf reminds Bilbo that his part in the story is important, but indeed only a part of it. That does not mean that his role in the war of the Ring was negligible. He is already a hero, but only one of them: the cause is not centred in his person, nor is it centred in anyone exclusively.

The story against the Ring is a narrative against the centralising and enthralling power of Sauron, whose strength is used only to his own advantages. In this story, there is room for great deeds and multiple heroes without one overshadowing the other. It is important also to remember that Bilbo did not achieve everything alone: he had help, as every hero in the saga of the Ring did.

Another criterion to elect a protagonist, according to Nikolajeva, is the frequent or constant presence of a character. It is undeniable that the story tends to focus on Frodo from the moment he leaves the Shire with the Ring, going to Rivendell, where he volunteers to be the definitive Ring-bearer. But when the fellowship breaks apart, Frodo disappears for many chapters, so his presence is not very frequent or constant. Moreover, Sam evolves as a character, and his role gradually becomes more central in the quest, so that he eventually is also called a *Ring-bearer*, as attested in the chapter "The Field of Cormallen", where the people cried: "*Praise them! The Ring-bearers, praise them with great praise!*".[15]

Nikolajeva also points out the first-person perspective and the focaliser, when a third-person narrator enters the mind of a character, normally the protagonist's. *The Lord of the Rings* is narrated in the third person, but the narrator often enters

14. Tolkien, J.R.R. *The Lord of the Rings*. Op. cit., pp. 351-352.
15. Id., p. 1248.

the mind of the characters, particularly when they are taken by doubt and fear. Initially, we see many of Frodo's internal conflicts; we follow Gollum's dichotomic personality and, after some time, Sam Gamgee also rises to protagonism in an ascending movement until the end of the story. Frodo, on the other hand, gradually becomes more silent, giving Sam the role of protagonist.

The last criterion Nikolajeva gives is the evolution, similar to the journey of the hero proposed by Joseph Campbell in his *The Hero with a Thousand Faces* (1949), in which a character goes through a process of development and change. This can be seen in most of the characters involved in the war of the Ring, because all the members of the fellowship experience this — Merry and Pippin even grow literally, their stature bearing the signs of their development.

Even the wise Gandalf changes and grows, evolving from Grey to White after his fight with the Balrog in Moria. Apart from the members of the Fellowship, other heroic friends show personal growth, like Faramir, Éowyn, and Théoden. Some, however, have more room to display their development, and in none this evolution is so emphasised as it is in Sam's case. That is why he will be the focus here.

Another significant feature of Tolkien's character-building is the importance of a supporting character. The narrative does not take away from Frodo his a priori, or apparent, role as the hero, but nor does it make him central in the story. The breaking of the fellowship favours the role of individual members, and it also aggrandises the humble, the ones who think less about themselves and more about the common good and their friends. Nikolajeva explains:

> It is basically impossible to construct a fairy-tale plot with one single character. Literary characters are normally depicted in their interaction with other characters, since our interest in fiction is primarily based on its treatment of human relationships.[16]

16. Nikolajeva, M. *The Rhetoric of Character in Children's Literature*. Op. cit., p. 110.

Her claim corroborates the purpose of this study, because friendship has a function to the end of the story, but it also plays an important role in its development. We can say that friendship contributes for the eucatastrophic outcome and that it brings happiness itself, being both a condition for the chief good and a symptom of it.[17]

Nine against nine

According to C.S. Lewis, friendship happens when two or more people see the same truth, but friendship lies especially in the question rather than in the answer to a question. That is, for people to become friends, it is necessary that they perceive the importance of a given subject, not that they agree with the answer: "In this kind of love, [... the question] 'Do you love me?' means *Do you see the same truth?* Or at least, 'Do you care about* the same truth?'".[18]

Let us go back to the Council of Elron, in Rivendell, where some representatives of the free peoples of Middle-earth, apart from Gandalf, had a long discussion, chaired by the Elf Elrond, about the story of the Ring, Gollum's whereabouts, and Sauron's plans to hold dominion over Middle-earth and enslave its inhabitants. It was known, then, that they were at war and that the Enemy had to be challenged.

Members of distinct peoples were present: Bilbo and Frodo; Gandalf; the Dwarves Glóin and his son, Gimli; several Elves of Rivendell and Legolas, an Elf from Mirkwood; the Men Boromir and Aragorn, and Sam, who participated secretly, without being invited, because he could not stay away from his Master. They had a common objective: to fight Sauron and his evil plan. They all brought with them the same truth about the war of the Ring. At that moment, their different races,

---

17. There is a correspondence in the biblical aphorism: "A faithful friend is a strong defense: and he that hath found such an one hath found a treasure" (Ecclesiasticus 6:14).

18. Lewis, C.S. *The Four Loves*. New York: Harcourt, Brace, 1960, p. 97.

origins, characteristics, and history did not matter as much as their shared truth. A friendly alliance was then formed, and they joined forces to fight the Enemy.

During the Council, Boromir suggested that the Ring be used to their advantage instead of destroyed. Elrond, however, warns that this would be a great danger:

> 'We cannot use the Ruling Ring. [...] It belongs to Sauron and was made by him alone, and is altogether evil. Its strength, Boromir, is too great for anyone to wield at will, save only those who have already a great power of their own. But for them it holds an even deadlier peril. The very desire of it corrupts the heart...'[19]

Gandalf also refuses to take the Ring himself and, with that, the hypothesis of keeping Sauron's object is discarded by all the attendants. In one of his letters, Tolkien explains what would have happened if Gandalf had taken the One Ring, hinting at the effect of the magical object in the Wise who had not yet been corrupted:

> Gandalf as Ring-Lord would have been far worse than Sauron. He would have remained 'righteous', but self-righteous. He would have continued to rule and order things for 'good', and the benefit of his subjects according to his wisdom (which was and would have remained great).
> [{...} In the margin Tolkien wrote: 'Thus while Sauron multiplied [illegible word] evil, he left "good" clearly distinguishable from it. Gandalf would have made good detestable and seem evil.'][20]

Frodo, in turn, felt the answer in his heart: he must take the Ring. the Hobbit then volunteers, and Elrond considers that a wise decision: 'I think that this task is appointed for you, Frodo; and that if you do not find a way, no one will.'[21]

Faced with Frodo's courage, Elrond acknowledges the

---

19. Tolkien, J.R.R. *The Lord of the Rings*. Op. cit., pp. 348-349.
20. Tolkien, J.R.R., Carpenter, H. (Org.), Tolkien, C. (Assist.). *The Letters of J.R.R. Tolkien*. Op. cit., Letter 246, pp. 332-333.
21. Tolkien, J.R.R. *The Lord of the Rings*. Op. cit., p. 353.

greatness of the Halflings. Sam, who could not endure seeing his Master leave without him, soon discloses that he had been eavesdropping. Elrond, then, grants him the right to go with Frodo, accomplishing the painful Quest.

After the Council, Elrond still has to decide how Frodo will set out. Merry and Pippin, upon finding that Sam will be Frodo's companion, become jealous, because they also want to go. The selfless act of these heroes is worth of attention. Frodo has his heart turned to a cause, having in his hands the well-being of his people and his friends. Merry and Pippin, just like Sam, have their hearts turned to one person: Frodo, their friend, who also grows in friendship with Sam along the journey. Throughout the saga, Merry and Pippin refine their refractoriness in favour of an idea, or a cause, as Frodo had done from the beginning, but they did not, as Baggins had not, put aside the personal love for the ones that gave them strength and a purpose to go on. This also happens with Sam in a process of development even more interesting.

After the Council, it was decided that Frodo and Sam would go southwards with Gandalf and six other friends, thus making *The Fellowship of the Ring*, with representatives of the free peoples of Middle-earth: Aragorn and Boromir representing Men; Legolas representing the Elves; Gimli, the Dwarves, and two other Hobbits, Merry and Pippin, who convinced Elrond to allow them to become members of the fellowship. The number of members should be nine, set in contrast to the nine Black Riders, the Nazgûl, or Ringwraiths, who had been corrupted by their Rings of Power and now served Sauron.

The Hobbits, it is to be noted, are the majority in the fellowship, and the ones who receive greater focus in the narrative, making room for us to study these characters more deeply. Maria Nikolajeva introduces us to a 1996 study by Ian Watt called Myths of *Modern Individualism*, which proposes a categorization of four major archetypal characters. The Robinson Crusoe archetype can be singled out as corresponding to all the members of *The Fellowship of the Ring*, or rather to

all characters actively involved in the war, but especially the
Hobbits:

> Robinson is one of the most prolific sources of children's literature,
> since this figure propagates liberation from parents, independence,
> individual development, and the spirit of enterprise. The novel
> is based on the same basic plot many scholars have observed in
> children's literature:[22] home (safe, but boring) — away (exciting,
> but dangerous) — return home. It empowers the character in an
> extraordinary situation, allowing degrees of growth and maturation
> more tangible and more profound than would be possible under
> normal conditions.[23]

Nikolajeva also talks about a five-step typology of
characters, according to Northrop Frye's 1977 concept of the
Displacement of Myth: *myth* (characters superior to human
beings and the laws of nature); *romance* (partially superior
characters, superior human beings, but inferior to gods, like
semi-gods); *high mimetic narrative* (presents human beings
who are superior to other human beings, but who are not
immortal, and not superior to the laws of nature); *low mimetic
narrative* (human beings who are neither superior, nor inferior
to other humans); *ironic narrative* (characters that lack
something of the "standard" adult, like children or people with
intellectual and physical limitations, or even other beings, like
animals).

It is possible to say that, in Tolkien's mythology, the
five types of character are present. The Valar and Valier are
representatives of the *myth*, being pure spirits, like angels,
created by Eru (God), and are themselves often considered
gods by Men. Their story is told in *The Silmarillion*, while in
The Lord of the Rings, even if some of their action is there, they

---

22. Nikolajeva's analysis focuses on children's literature, but Watt's archetypes are
present in all genres, including the fantasy in which *The Lord of the Rings* is placed,
pervaded by the marvellous and the mythic, and which is commonly associated to
children by those who have a superficial notion of the work.
23. Nikolajeva, M. *The Rhetoric of Character in Children's Literature*. Op. cit., pp.
42-43.

are not explicitly present in the narrative, and it is necessary to know deeply Tolkien's mythology to detect them in the saga of the Ring.

The Maiar, like Gandalf, Saruman, and Sauron himself could be circumscribed in the romance type, being superior to Men but inferior to the Valar, whom they serve. The Elves are part of a *high mimetic narrative*, being Men's archetypes, associated with the arts, nature, and wisdom, but they are immortal while the concrete world of Nature exists and, thus, also bear some aspects of the *romance* category.

Men, in turn, like Aragorn and Boromir, could fit the *low mimetic narrative* category, representing our own humanity of the Primary World.[24] Finally, Hobbits like Frodo, Bilbo, Sam, Merry, Pippin, and even Gollum — of a close origin to the Hobbits — would be representatives of the *ironic narrative* because, while a branch of Mankind, they are considered less relevant among the peoples of Middle-earth. Called Halflings, not even the Ents knew about their existence, and they were forgotten by the wisest, like Saruman. Gandalf, however, did not underrate them, and gave them voice and a great responsibility in the destruction of the Ring.

Nikolajeva highlights a peculiarity of the categories proposed by Frye: they can happen diachronically or synchronically, that is, they can either traverse time in History, or can coexist in a given time. Tolkien is singular in this aspect: he brings several categories to *the same work*, and that is noticeable because it is present, in a way, since *The Hobbit*, which is considered children's literature.

> According to Frye, contemporary Western literature has reached the ironic stage, at which most of the characters we meet in novels are weak, disillusioned men and women. This is only true of quality literature, since most formulaic fiction operates within the romantic mode (which in Frye's terminology includes romance, adventure,

---

24. Even though they are descendants of the Númenóreans, stronger and more powerful Humans than the rest. Thus, they could also somewhat fit the *high mimetic narrative*.

fantasy, etc.), and at least some contemporary adult fiction still uses mimetic modes. Furthermore, Frye's model does not presuppose linear development but is formed as a cycle, which means that after the ironic stage, a new mythic stage can be expected.[25]

Tolkien's fantasy, particularly his two greatest books published in life, *The Hobbit* and *The Lord of the Rings*, subverted this limited concept of fantasy, which brought only heroes of *myth, romance*, and, rarely, *mimetic narrative*. Tolkien gives a prominent role to The Hobbits, considered "minor" beings (ironic narrative) but who are actually much more valiant — from the perspective of their character, of the essential virtues of a good man, according to Aristotelian ethics — and are the greatest heroes of their adventures.[26]

However, each member of the Fellowship of the Ring has an important role in the story. And not only they, but also other characters who appear along the way. Even Gollum, as we saw in the previous chapter, exerts some protagonism and is, ironically, necessary for the happy ending of the saga, unwillingly saving the whole of Middle-earth. All this gives a dash of postmodernity to Tolkien's work, in which victory against evil does not always come by the deeds of the good ones, the heroes.

That does not mean that the central characters are repulsive, or that they do not provide us readers with elements for self-identification. On the contrary, even Gollum arouses empathy and compassion, and the other heroes bring one or another element with which the reader can identify, their successes, anxieties, and especially their failures. *The Lord of the Rings* shows that it is in failure that one supports the other, and the victory in the war of the Ring occurs in it: it is in failure, and because of it, that the Tolkienian heroes become friends.

But the eucatastrophic ending is not the end of their

25. Nikolajeva, M. *The Rhetoric of Character in Children's Literature*. Op. cit., p. 27.

26. The Dwarves are also highly prominent in *The Hobbit*; in *The Silmarillion*, they shift from low mimetic to ironic narrative, being the illegitimate children of Eru.

friendship. After the destruction of the Ring, the narrator shows a sequence of events, even adventures, in each one's journey back home, keeping their bonds of friendship. According to Aristotle, we need friends in good and bad fortune, because "in misfortune we need help, in prosperity we need people to live with and to do good to; for we wish to do good".[27]

Over the next few pages, we will find out more about the peoples represented in *The Fellowship of the Ring* and their importance for the story.

Elves and Dwarves

The least probable friendship of *The Fellowship of the Ring* is that between the Elf Legolas and the Dwarf Gimli. Both peoples had estrangements that dated back to the First Age of Middle-earth's history and which ensued mortal battles between them.

But the origins of that disagreement can be traced back to a time even before the First Age, when Elves and Men had not yet awakened in the world. It is told in the mythology that the Elves are called Eru Ilúvatar's Firstborn, and the Men are the Followers. The Dwarves, in turn, were originally created by the Vala Aulë, who could not await the coming of the Children of Ilúvatar and created his own offspring. So *The Silmarillion* says:

> And the voice of Ilúvatar said to Aulë: 'Thy offer I accepted even as it was made. Dost thou not see that these things have now a life of their own, and speak with their own voices? [...] Even as I gave being to the thoughts of the Ainur at the beginning of the World, so now I have taken up thy desire and given to it a place therein [...]. They shall sleep now in the darkness under stone, and shall not come forth until the Firstborn have awakened upon Earth [...]. But when the time comes I will awaken them, and they shall be to thee as children; and often strife shall arise between thine and mine, the children of my adoption and the children of my choice.'[28]

---

27. Aristotle. *The Nicomachean Ethics*. Op. cit., p. 314.
28. Tolkien, J.R.R. *The Silmarillion*. London: HarperCollins, 1999, pp. 37-38. Emphasis added.

Magnus Orn Thordarson, in his article "The Theme of Friendship in J.R.R. Tolkien's *The Lord of the Rings*", claims that even in the Council of Elrond the differences between the two peoples are evident, when the Dwarf Glóin recalls being incarcerated by the Elves of Mirkwood, whence Legolas came. Gandalf, however, stops him: "Pray, do not interrupt, my good Glóin. That was a regrettable misunderstanding, long set right. If all the grievances that stand between Elves and Dwarves are to be brought up here, we may as well abandon this Council".[29]

Thordarson calls attention to the fact that Gimli, son of Glóin, starts to change his hostile behaviour towards the Elves when he goes to Lothlórien. The Dwarf is enchanted by the Lady of Lórien, Galadriel, and, as a parting gift, he asks her for one strand of her golden hair. Galadriel gives him not one, but three,[30] which Gimli keeps as a relic, and she foretells that, if hope should not fail, Gimli's hand would flow with gold, but gold would not have dominion over him. From then on, Legolas and Gimli leave the elven kingdom closer, and as friends.

The friendship between them grows to the point that they agree to explore together the Forest of Fangorn, a dream of Legolas's, and the Glittering Caves of Helm's Deep, something Gimli desired. At the end of the war of the Ring, they do fulfil that promise and travel together. Such an agreement shows how their friendship got close enough to arouse in them the desire to know each other's world and take interest in things they had rejected for a long time. For a common cause, Legolas and Gimli overcome the estrangement of their ancestors, symbolising the forgiveness and alliance between their peoples.

---

29. Tolkien, J.R.R. *The Lord of the Rings*. Op. cit., pp. 332-333.
30. This seemingly trivial act is a valuable one. Galadriel is a powerful Elf, and her hair had been admired and coveted since the First Age.

The Followers

The two Men who take part in the Fellowship of the Ring are Aragorn, heir to the throne of Gondor, and Boromir, son of the steward of that realm. But Aragorn is not introduced as a future king: his first appearance in *The Lord of the Rings* happens at an inn called The Prancing Pony, located in Bree, and he is introduced by his nickname "Strider". He initially approaches Frodo and the other Hobbits at The Prancing Pony in a mysterious, sinister way. The innkeeper Barliman Butterbur describes him:

> He is one of the wandering folk – Rangers we call them. He seldom talks: not but what he can tell a rare tale when he has the mind. He disappears for a month, or a year, and then he pops up again. [...] What his right name is I've never heard: but he's known round here as Strider. Goes about at a great pace on his long shanks; though he don't tell nobody what cause he has to hurry.[31]

Aragorn hides his identity as a protection against Sauron's vengeance, seeing that his ancestor, Isildur, was the son of Elendil, founder of Gondor and the one who took the Ring from Sauron's hand, bearing it after the war of the Last Alliance. During his childhood, after his father Arathorn died, Aragorn was sent to Rivendell, and was there brought up by the Elves, who protected and instructed him as their own child. When he grew up, he learned about his origins and became a wanderer and, at Gandalf's request, started protecting the Hobbits. That is why he approached them at the inn.

After trying to persuade Frodo to let him accompany them to Rivendell, where the Council was to take place, Butterbur remembered that Gandalf had left a letter, addressed to Frodo, which should have been sent to the Shire before the Hobbit left, explaining that, should he find Strider, he could trust him because he was a friend and would help him.

---

31. Tolkien, J.R.R. *The Lord of the Rings*. Op. cit., p. 205.

'I believed that you were a friend before the letter came,' he [Frodo] said, 'or at least I wished to. You have frightened me several times tonight, but never in the way that servants of the Enemy would, or so I imagine. I think one of his spies would – well, seem fairer and feel fouler, if you understand.'

'I see,' laughed Strider. '[...] *All that is gold does not glitter, not all those who wander are lost.*'[32]

Several times, Tolkien's legendarium shows that a neat appearance is not always evidence of goodness, corroborating the idea that friendship is founded first and foremost upon the character of the individuals. Frodo and the other Hobbits accept Strider's company to Rivendell, where the Ring-bearer would be chosen.

By then, Gondor had been ruled by stewards since the last king died. At that time, the steward was Denethor II, Boromir and Faramir's father. He favoured his firstborn, who seemed to be, like him, very much attached to the rule of the realm. Faramir, the younger brother, had a more honest and less greedy heart, being Gandalf's friend, even though he did want to please his father. When Denethor finds that Boromir had died, his sanity starts deteriorating until he decides to burn himself and his youngest when he sees Faramir returning wounded by the enemies' attack. After this attempted incineration, Faramir is in grave danger, but eventually recovers in the Houses of Healing. Denethor, however, commits suicide by throwing himself into a pyre, and Gondor's rule is temporarily vacant.

Aragorn was unsure whether he should take the crown of Gondor to himself, given that he was ashamed of his ancestors' mistakes. The ranger of the North was a good and virtuous Man and was on friendly terms with Elves, Hobbits, Dwarves, and especially Gandalf. Without them, he would not have been able to overcome Sauron's persecution, and he needed his friends as much as they needed Aragorn's courage and discernment to defeat Evil.

---

32. Id., p. 224.

But another kind of love, different from friendship, drove him in his fight against Sauron: Eros. In Rivendell, now an adult, he fell in love with the Elf Arwen,[33] Elrond's daughter. The biggest trouble with such a love comes from the fact that the Elves do not die, at least not while Nature exists, unless they are murdered or relinquish their immortality. Arwen was willing to give up her immortality to be with her love, but her father, Elrond, was opposed to that, even though he loved Aragorn as a son.[34]

Arwen, at last, followed her own desire, however much she loved her father, and decided to become a mortal and Aragorn's spouse. When he learned that, Elrond told the Dúnadan:

> "'[…] Therefore, though I love you, I say to you: Arwen Undómiel shall not diminish her life's grace for less cause. She shall not be the bride of any Man less than the King of both Gondor and Arnor. To me then even our victory can bring only sorrow and parting – but to you hope of joy for a while […].'"[35]

In the eucatastrophic ending of the saga, the Ring is destroyed, Aragorn is crowned Elessar, king of Gondor, and marries Arwen, as both had desired, despite the consequences. Their story, however, is told in a few lines throughout the book, and only in the appendices do we learn it in more detail. Thus, the Eros type of love is present in a less prominent way than Affection and, especially, Friendship, which is more emphasised in the Hobbits. In a letter, Tolkien says the following:

> […] I regard the tale of Arwen and Aragorn as the most important of the Appendices; it is pan of the essential story, and is only placed

---

33. Strictly speaking, she is considered a "Half-Elven", having the Elvish and Human blood of her ancestors.
34. In the appendices to *The Lord of the Rings* (Tolkien, 2008, p. 1353), it is said that "[…] But to the children of Elrond a choice was also appointed: to pass with him from the circles of the world; or if they remained to become mortal and die in Middle-earth. For Elrond, therefore, all chances of the War of the Ring were fraught with sorrow".
35. Tolkien, J.R.R. *The Lord of the Rings*. Op. cit., p. 1391.

so, because it could not be worked into the main narrative without destroying its structure: which is planned to be 'hobbito-centric', that is, primarily a study of the ennoblement (or sanctification) of the humble.[36]

Such a concept is complemented in another letter by the Professor:

[...] this last great Tale [...] is seen mainly through the eyes of Hobbits: [...] because the last Tale is to exemplify most clearly a recurrent theme: the place in 'world polities' of the unforeseen and unforeseeable acts of will, and deeds of virtue of the apparently small, ungreat, forgotten in the places of the Wise and Great (good as well as evil).[37]

A Hobbito-centric view

In the Prologue to *The Lord of the Rings*, we learn that the adventures told in *The Hobbit* and *The Lord of the Rings* are contained in *The Red Book of Westmarch*, starting with Bilbo's stories, who then passed it on to Frodo, who handed it to Sam and his descendants afterwards. The story brought the Halfling's view to the readers. It is suggested that *The Lord of the Rings* was, in fact, a translation of the *Red Book*, as can be found in the frontispiece of the book: "*The Lord of the Rings* translated from the Red Book of Westmarch by John Ronald Reuel Tolkien: herein is set forth the history of the War of the Ring and the Return of the King as seen by the Hobbits".

Still in the Prologue, the Hobbits are thus described:

Hobbits are an unobtrusive but very ancient people, more numerous formerly than they are today; for they love peace and quiet and good tilled earth [...]. They do not and did not understand or like machines more complicated than a forge-bellows, a water-mill, or a hand-loom [...].

---

36. Tolkien, J.R.R., Carpenter, H. (Org.), Tolkien, C. (Assist.). *The Letters of J.R.R. Tolkien*. Op. cit., Letter 181, p. 237.
37. Id., Letter 131, p. 160.

> For they are a little people, smaller than Dwarves [...].
> Their faces were as a rule good-natured rather than beautiful, broad, bright-eyed, red-cheeked, with mouths apt to laughter, and to eating and drinking. And laugh they did, and eat, and drink, often and heartily, being fond of simple jests at all times, and of six meals a day (when they could get them). They were hospitable and delighted in parties, and in presents, which they gave away freely and eagerly accepted.[38]

We can find many characteristics of children in the Hobbits by looking at their size, their semblance, and eating habits, for instance. The book represents a people with several features of the Child Archetype, particularly innocence and selflessness. The author proceeds:

> It is plain indeed that in spite of later estrangement Hobbits are relatives of ours: far nearer to us than Elves, or even than Dwarves [...]. But what exactly our relationship is can no longer be discovered.[39]

When Merry and Pippin get lost in Fangorn Forest, they have an interesting dialogue with Treebeard, the oldest and wisest of all the Ents:

> '[...] But anyway you do not seem to fit in anywhere!'
> 'We always seem to have got left out of the old lists, and the old stories,' said Merry. 'Yet we've been about for quite a long time. We're hobbits.'
> '[...] Who calls you hobbits, though? That does not sound Elvish to me. Elves made all the old words: they began it.'
> 'Nobody else calls us hobbits; we call ourselves that,' said Pippin.[40]

The fact that Merry and Pippin strayed away from the Fellowship, after being captured by the Uruk-hais who were following Saruman's orders, favoured the strengthening of ties between them and contributed for a more active participation

---

38. Tolkien, J.R.R. *The Lord of the Rings*. Op. cit., pp. 1-2.
39. Id., pp. 2-3.
40. Id., p. 605.

in the war. If that had not happened, the Ents would not have marched to Isengard to fight Saruman's army, defeating the Wizard's dominion over that territory.

According to Maria Nikolajeva, in *The Rhetoric of Character in Children's Literature*, friends may be helpers or quest objects in a story. Besides mustering forces against Saruman, Merry and Pippin were another reason for Aragorn, Legolas, and Gimli to continue their mission, because they were looking for the two Hobbits that had been taken. In that search, they came across Gandalf, now the White, and they stayed together until they reached the realm of Rohan where they would later join forces with King Théoden.

The two Halflings would also be remembered by their great deeds. Merry joins Éowyn, King Théoden's niece, to fight in the Battle of the Pelennor Fields, even without the King's permission, and he helps her defeat the Witch-king of Angmar, Lord of the Nazgûl. Pippin also plays an important role in the final battle, killing a Troll-chief in the Battle of the Morannon, the last one in the War of the Ring.

The development of the Hobbits shows that the Halfling's nobility of character aggrandises them, and often makes them stronger than the Wise and the Great. This claim is corroborated by the following statement by Gandalf, in the White Council: "'Many are the strange chances of the world,' said Mithrandir, 'and help oft shall come from the hands of the weak when the Wise falter'".[41]

Two poles of a war

Tolkien's works are often criticised because of the depth of its characters and the portrayal of Good and Evil. The author talks about it in one of his letters:

> But the Elves are *not* wholly good or in the right. [...] In their way the Men of Gondor were similar: a withering people whose only

---

41. Tolkien, J.R.R. *The Silmarillion*. Op. cit., p. 362.

'hallows' were their tombs. *But in any case this is a tale about a war*, and if war is allowed [...] it is not much good complaining that all the people on one side are against those on the other. Not that I have made even this issue quite so simple: there are Saruman, and Denethor, and Boromir; and there are treacheries and strife even among the Orcs.[42]

Others claim that his works are unrealistic in portraying Good through virtuous characters who never fail and, therefore, do not bear any resemblance to the Primary World. However, one can actually find holes in such arguments: first, as it was mentioned here, even Sauron's opponents display failures and contradictions; second, if the virtuous individual exists in our Primary World, even though with human flaws and weaknesses, the trust in the other still endures.

Besides that, as the Professor said in his letter, the story is about a war and polarization is, therefore, *sine qua non*. The choice between Good and Evil lies in our reader's perception, according to our own paradigms — our family, personal, social, and historical values, for instance — not to mention the hints the very text gives us: Sauron, lord of the Rings of Power, is called the Enemy by the Fellowship.

Jessica Yates discusses the criticism to the portrayal of Evil in *The Lord of the Rings*:

Tolkien's view of Evil has also been criticised. However, it is appropriate for supernatural genres to depict creatures of ultimate evil, like aliens and monsters, whereas fictions set in the real world cannot do this. So we need fantasy to experience the extremes of Good and Evil, testing real life against the fantasy. Sauron, in his desire to conquer and control the world, is not very different from a real-world dictator: it is his methods which count.[43]

---

42. Tolkien, J.R.R., Carpenter, H. (Org.), Tolkien, C. (Assist.). *The Letters of J.R.R. Tolkien*. Op. cit., Letter 154, p. 197. Emphasis added on 'But in any case... war'.
43. Yates, J. *Tolkien as a Writer for Young Adults*
<https://www.tolkiensociety.org/app/uploads/2016/11/Tolkien-as-a-Writer-for-Young-Adults.pdf> [Accessed 24 April, 2020].

The first time a word related to enemy appears in *The Lord of the Rings*, in the form of "foe", is right in the Prologue, when it talks about the nature of the Hobbits:

> They were, if it came to it, difficult to daunt or to kill; and they were, perhaps, so unwearyingly fond of good things not least because they could, when put to it, do without them, and could survive rough handling by grief, *foe*, or weather in a way that astonished those who did not know them well and looked no further than their bellies and their well-fed faces.[44]

Further on, still in the prologue, when narrating Bilbo's story with the Ring, the word appears again, now in the form of "enemy":

> There Gollum crouched at bay, smelling and listening; and Bilbo was tempted to slay him with his sword. But pity stayed him, and though he kept the ring, in which his only hope lay, he would not use it to help him kill the wretched creature at a disadvantage. In the end, gathering his courage, he leaped over Gollum in the dark, and fled away down the passage, pursued by his *enemy*'s cries of hate and despair: *Thief, thief! Baggins! We hates it for ever!*[45]

These two examples — "foe" and "enemy" — bear a more general sense of an "adversary". For the Hobbits, the enemy could be anyone who attacked them. For Gollum, it was whoever ill-treated him, whether it was someone fair or unfair, from an ethical point of view.

However, the Enemy, with a capital letter, referring to one specific creature, Sauron, appears a little later, in the beginning of the chapter "The Shadow of the Past":

> There were rumours of strange things happening in the world outside. [...] Frodo often met strange dwarves of far countries, seeking refuge in the West. They were troubled, and some spoke in whispers of the Enemy and of the Land of Mordor.[46]

---

44. Tolkien, J.R.R. *The Lord of the Rings*. Op. cit., p. 7. Emphasis added.
45. Id., p. 16. Emphasis added on 'enemy'.
46. Id., p. 57. Emphasis added.

From then on, the term Enemy is also a proper name, referring to one single concrete being. It is from that moment on, also, that evil is defined in the story, being placed upon Sauron and his allies. On the other hand, as Tolkien claimed in the aforementioned letter, Evil could be found elsewhere, for instance: enemy against enemy (the wizard Saruman against Sauron; Orcs against other Orcs); an enemy among friends (Denethor trying to burn his own son; Boromir attacking Frodo); the enemy of one's own self (Gollum against Sméagol; Frodo in his final failure).

Sauron trusted the dividing power of Evil to turn allies into enemies during the War of the Ring. The Enemy's central point, however, is not exactly within himself, but in the object he devised. By creating it, Sauron gains a dominating force by wielding the Ring but, to make this happen, he needed to convey to the object much of his own power, as Tolkien explains in another letter:

> But even if he did not wear it, that power existed and was in 'rapport' with himself: he was not 'diminished'. Unless some other seized it and became possessed of it. If that happened, the new possessor could (if sufficiently strong and heroic by nature) challenge Sauron, become master of all [...]. There was another weakness: if the One Ring was actually unmade, annihilated, then its power would be dissolved, Sauron's own being would be diminished to vanishing point, and he would be reduced to a shadow, a mere memory of malicious will.[47]

The book presents, then, two wars that had to be fought: the free peoples against Sauron and his slaves, and the internal war against one's own self, especially the battle between Sauron, the devisor of the magical object, and the Ring-bearers. In this sense, the presence of Isildur's Bane among the characters brings to the surface what Nikolajeva calls the "Little Mermaid" archetype. In the original tale, she is dangerous to

---

47. Tolkien, J.R.R., Carpenter, H. (Org.), Tolkien, C. (Assist.). *The Letters of J.R.R. Tolkien*. Op. cit., Letter 131, pp. 153-154.

her own self.[48] In *The Lord of the Rings*, all the characters, to a greater or lesser extent, represent a danger to their own selves, according to their attachment to the Ring, particularly when one bears it.

However, the effect of the magical object is augmented according to the individual's character. Besides that, the force of its actions conforms to the amount of time a person bears it and is also in accordance with Sauron's power. It took Sméagol, for instance, who already led a vile life, only a little time until he took his friend Déagol's life by coveting the Ring. Frodo, in turn, spent eighteen years with the Ring but only in the last one did he feel its pression more clearly, when Sauron's power started to really get stronger. It is possible to say, then, that the Ring, an extension of Sauron's personality, acts as a catalyst character, around which the plot tends to revolve.

Paradoxically, the Ring both hinders and helps the free Men. It is often by using the magical object that the characters can avoid being caught by Sauron. Frodo uses the artefact to escape from Boromir, for instance, and Sam avoids the Orcs when rescuing Frodo, after finding out that his master had not been killed by Shelob's poison, as he previously thought. Such a contradiction in the nature of the Ring reflects the effects of Evil in the work, which is characterised by division and betrayal. Besides that, the text subtly suggests that other powers, benign and more powerful than Sauron's, acted in the War of the Ring, without eschewing the strength and courage of the free peoples.

The end of Tolkien's novel is eucatastrophic, a word which is often mistaken as the mere use of a *deus ex machina* ("god from the machine", in Latin), which indicates an unexpected solution for a problem different from what the plot constructs from the beginning. Eucatastrophe, in turn, is the good catastrophe, the happy ending which coheres with the possibilities and elements already present in the novel and based on its principles.

---

48. Nikolajeva, M. *The Rhetoric of Character in Children's Literature*. Op. cit., p. 116.

The possibility of the Ruling Ring being destroyed always existed, even though there were several obstacles for that to happen. By chance, divine providence, the actions among friends, good deeds of heroes involved in the saga, and the very self-destructive nature of Evil, Sauron is defeated in the heart of Mount Doom, in whose fire Gollum falls with his precious.

Chapter Five

Equals in virtue

Aristotle claims that perfect friendship is only possible between those who are equals in virtue. However, we have demonstrated that, in the saga of the Ring, all characters undergo a process of development, either evolving into virtue or declining into vice. Equality, therefore, is not immediately established in most of the heroes we have studied.

We are now going to reflect about the practice of virtue, so necessary for friendship to approach the one considered perfect and to move away from the ones considered incidental, in the Aristotelian conception. To do that, our attention will turn especially to the friendship between unequals, how it is configured in these cases, and how it can be changed, that is, how inequality can be effaced and friendship become perfect — or at least close to it, given that, in the Christian ethics upon which Tolkien was based, a common man cannot be wholly good, but, however virtuous (a condition for one to be a good friend), one would still have some flaws.[1]

Among the examples of friendship between unequals, in his *Nicomachean Ethics* Aristotle points out the one that ensues between those who rule and those who obey. Such a friendship seems important here because it is exactly the one between Frodo and Sam — not to mention others, such as Gandalf towards the Fellowship, and then Aragorn, in Gandalf's absence and as king etc.

The two Hobbits have a Master-Subject relationship: Sam is Frodo's gardener, and he is the son of the Gaffer, Hamfast

---

1. See Luke 18:19: "And Jesus said unto him, Why callest thou me good? none is good, save one, that is, God".

Gamgee, who works for Frodo. There is a considerable age gap between them,[2] Baggins being fifteen years older than his gardener.

According to Aristotle, the friendship between master and subject is normally of the incidental type, and the one in a superior position may look for someone in an inferior position either for utility or pleasure, but seldom would both occur simultaneously in a single individual. The good, virtuous man would be both useful and pleasant, but would not be friends with someone in a superior position unless one were also superior in virtue, which is, according to the Greek philosopher, very hard to find.

We can see that Sam and Frodo's relationship, at least in the beginning, is one of the rare cases in which both the ruler and the subject are already virtuous people but, due to their social imbalance, perfect friendship is not immediately established. Their relationship is, of course, cordial and friendly, given that Frodo does not show distant behaviour towards Sam. On the contrary, Baggins is both close and accessible to him. They are friends, in a way, but it cannot be said, in principle, that their friendship is close to the perfect one, as it becomes by the end of the story.

A common cause — the struggle to destroy the Ring — is necessary for each of them to practice their good habits, making them even more virtuous, equalising them through virtue and making the Master-Gardener relationship less evident. That does not happen immediately but takes time and a long way for the individual's journey to transform them in heroes.

Aristotle claims that in all friendships implying inequality. His "principle of proportion", in which "equality is effected and friendship preserved"[3] between individuals in unequal position governs Frodo and Sam's case. The better party is to

2. Considering that Hobbits live longer than we do, about one hundred years. A Hobbit comes of age at 33, and their adolescence happened in their twenties, and is called, therefore, "tweens".

3. Aristotle. *The Nicomachean Ethics*, trans. by F. H. Peters, 10 edn. London: Kegan Paul, Trench, Trübner & Co., 1906, p. 284.

be understood as the more virtuous one and, therefore, also the more useful, because it serves the other in a better way. In this case, we can say that Frodo, being more mature, is also more virtuous than Sam in the beginning of the saga. However, this situation changes along the process as Sam becomes more mature, particularly in making decisions, while Frodo becomes less active due to his burden, the Ring, and the responsibility of his mission.

The gardener, thus, becomes more useful, and Frodo in a way becomes more dependent on him, but still being virtuous and having his grave importance as Ring-bearer. The devotional love Sam has for his master becomes stronger, but Frodo's admiration for his companion also grows to the point that the inequality between them becomes almost insignificant, even though Sam still tries to serve his master, even after the destruction of the Ring.

That specific issue is solved in the end of the saga, when Sam is torn between his mission of taking care of Frodo and building his own, independent life. Sam finds out that his master will depart with Bilbo and the Elves from the Grey Havens to the Undying Lands, but despite his request, Frodo cannot take him: 'Do not be too sad, Sam. *You cannot be always torn in two. You will have to be one and whole*, for many years. You have so much to enjoy and to be, and to do.'[4] From that moment, Sam is freed from his obligation to serve Frodo, and the inequality disappears at last, with his master's approval. At the end of his life, however, after Rosie, Sam's wife, died, it is believed that he met Frodo in the Undying Lands. Their friendship was not over with the end of the Subject-Master obligation: it endured to their life's end, being very close to that which is considered the perfect kind of friendship.

For the friendship, being based on these motives [pleasure and utility], is dissolved whenever they fail to obtain that for the sake of which they made friends; for it was not the other's self that each

4. Tolkien, J.R.R. *The Lord of the Rings*. London: HarperCollins, 2008, p. 1346.

loved, but something which he had, and which is not apt to endure; for which reason these friendships also are not apt to endure. But friendship based on character, being pure, is likely to last.[5]

It is important to recall some concepts about equality in Aristotle, establishing a relationship between justice and Christian charity, according to the initial purpose of this study concerning its theoretical foundations, which agrees with Tolkien's works. In the Greek conception, the equality of justice is merit-based, while friendship, in personal and intimate context, focused on charity, is based on the exchange of how much one can wish well and do good to another person.

Aristotle talks about a possible contradiction in such a dynamics of friendship, because if the purpose is to help a friend develop his or her character, when it reached the necessary degree of virtue, the person would be like a deity, not an equal anymore, and would not need friendship. However, the philosopher claims that friendship is important both in adversity and in prosperity, the latter being justified by the necessity of doing good to others. By extension, we can understand such a claim from a material and also a moral point of view, in which virtuous people rejoice in the presence of the other and in the practice of mutual good.

This impasse is more consistently solved within the field of theology. According to Tolkien — even though he rejected allegory in his works — "*The Lord of the Rings* is of course a fundamentally religious and Catholic work; unconsciously so at first, but consciously in the revision".[6] Because of that, the religious concepts of Tolkien's fiction are added to those of classical philosophy.

The concept of Christian friendship and the one proposed by Aristotelian ethics have nuances that are differentiated, or would be transcended, in the sphere of faith, in the transition

---

5. Aristotle. *The Nicomachean Ethics*. Op. cit., pp. 286–287.
6. Tolkien, J.R.R., Carpenter, H. (Org.), Tolkien, C. (Assist.). *The Letters of J.R.R. Tolkien*. London: HarperCollins, 2006, Letter 142, p. 172.

from philosophy to theology. In Christianity, friendship is based on trinitary love — the Father, the Son, and the Holy Ghost — a single God who is also a community/communion, that is, who has always loved, because it springs from himself, generating another person (and another one). Since this characteristic is intrinsic to the divine being, in which the Christian God has a relational structure, there is friendship even from the Lord towards Men — however immeasurable the difference between one and the other — because loving is inherent to the divine essence.

Tolkien brought to his work the ideal of Christian holiness, even though he only became aware of that in the revision of *The Lord of the Rings*. The holy soul sees perfect friendship in God who, as we have said, is trinitarian, having in Christ, the Son, a model for Men.

The Gospel of John deals with friendship from the theological point of view in a more emphatic way. The maxim of Christ's teaching is found in there:

> This is my commandment, that ye love one another, as I have loved you. Greater love hath no man than this, that a man lay down his life for his friends. Ye are my friends, if ye do whatsoever I command you. Henceforth I call you not servants; for the servant knoweth not what his lord doeth: but I have called you friends; for all things that I have heard of my Father I have made known unto you.[7]

It is noticeable that Christ warns that friendship lies, in this case, in inequality, because there is a lord-servant relationship between him and Men: "Ye are my friends, if ye do whatsoever I *command* you". According to Christian faith, Jesus is God; thus, the inequality between him and Men will always be a fact. But he is also incarnated in human nature, he makes himself one of us, and equality, so necessary for friendship, is also possible and real in this relationship: "I call you not servants; for the servant knoweth not what his lord doeth: but

---

7. John 15: 12-15.

I have called you friends; for all things that I have heard of my Father I have made known unto you".

Frodo and Sam have a lord-servant relationship which can be connected to Christ's teaching by analogy, kept in proportion, and using the principle of applicability, which enables one to present one's interpretation of a non-allegorical work. Sam regards Frodo as a master — it is, indeed, the title he uses to address him, as does Gollum. He sees in Bilbo's heir someone in a superior position not only from a social point of view, but also from the intellectual and ethical one. For Sam, Frodo knows more than him and also has a superior moral demeanour: it is Baggins who gives his life for his friends, according to the Christian commandment and, because of that, he shows more love and, consequently, is worthier of being loved. More than mere chance, Frodo's volunteering to bear the Ring was a consequence of his knowing, deep down, that he was the chosen one. Sam sees in Frodo an ideal of life and, for him, the mission of serving him was obvious.

Gamgee is not himself a highly ambitious person and, therefore, the Ring's effect on him is less intense, even when he bears it for a short period of time. The gardener knows his place and simply plays his own role well. This is the key feature of the paradoxical Tolkienian ethics, particularly *The Lord of the Rings*: the humbler and "lesser" a character is, the greater he is before the others.[8] According to Christ's teachings, the lesser one, the one who follows their masters — God himself — shall be the greatest of all. Tolkien conceives and applies well such an ethics in his literary work, even though unconsciously.

But the author does not eschew the importance of the wise and the great. In fact, he conjoins the concepts: "without the high and noble the simple and vulgar is utterly mean; and without the simple and ordinary the noble and heroic is

---

8. "So the last shall be first, and the first last: for many be called, but few chosen" (Matthew 20:16).

meaningless".[9] Frodo, in a way, has both sides: he is one of the Halflings, with the simplicity of the Hobbits, but he also has a great soul and received education, given that he learned from Bilbo the elvish tongue and acquired advanced knowledge about the stories of Middle-earth.

Sam is fascinated by everything Frodo represents and wants, with him, to learn and live such knowledge. His fidelity takes him far in his adventures: following his master, the son of the Gaffer becomes the master himself, unknowingly. He gradually becomes Frodo's equal, then inequality disappears, and a friendship close to the perfect type emerges.

We can say that the Aristotelian concept of perfect friendship, founded on virtue, may extend from the private context — with mutual benevolence — to the public sphere — involving justice and merit. The *Nicomachean Ethics* focus essentially on studying human behaviour from a political point of view, but two of its ten chapters are dedicated to friendship. In these chapters, Aristotle places this kind of love primarily in the private sphere and claims that it should be transferred to collectivity as well. By progressing in virtue, the lesser evolves from the perspective of social justice — which, however, depends on other factors — and of private friendship.

This is evidenced when Sam returns to the Shire and, later, becomes the Mayor for many years. He is also Frodo's heir — who did not have children — and is responsible, with his family, for continuing the narrative in the first volume of *The Red Book of Westmarch*, which Bilbo had started. Because he evolved in virtue, becoming a mature citizen with a strong and good character, Sam also was decisive in the public sphere, remaining Mayor for 55 years, seven terms in a row. Kept in proportion, his story is similar to Aragorn's, which is also characterised by an individual who undertakes a quest, serving the others, until he becomes the King.

9. Tolkien, J.R.R., Carpenter, H. (Org.), Tolkien, C. (Assist.). *The Letters of J.R.R. Tolkien*. Op. cit., Letter 131, p. 160.

Those who beyond other men set their hearts on noble deeds are
welcomed and praised by all; but if all men were vieing with each
other in the pursuit of what is noble, and were straining every nerve
to act in the noblest possible manner, the result would be that both
the wants of the community would be perfectly satisfied, and at
the same time each individually would win the greatest of all good
things — for virtue is that.[10]

Olórin and Nienna

The Istar Gandalf plays a crucial role in the victory in the War of
the Ring, and his participation goes beyond his wizard powers.
He contributes, especially, in ensuring that one of the most
important virtues be practiced by Frodo: mercy. Inasmuch as
friendship is concerned, we have briefly considered all the free
peoples of Middle-earth who were present in the Fellowship of
the Ring, whose nine members would oppose the nine Nazgûl.
The ninth member, Gandalf, was not from Middle-earth, but
from Aman, the Undying Lands, because he was a Maia. He
must, therefore, be studied more closely, along with the Valië
Nienna, of whom he was a pupil.

In *The Silmarillion*, it is said that the original name of the
wizard was Olórin,[11] in the elvish language Quenya, spoken by
the Elves that dwelled in Valinor. He was considered the wisest
among the Maiar, and dwelled in Lórien, the lands of Irmo, the
Vala of Dreams, but he would often go to Nienna's house,

> [...] and of her he learned pity and patience [...] he was the friend
> of all the Children of Ilúvatar, and took pity on their sorrows; and
> those who listened to him awoke from despair and put away the
> imaginations of darkness.[12]

---

10. Aristotle. *The Nicomachean Ethics*. Op. cit., p. 306.
11. The word *olori*, in Elvish, corresponded to the concept of "dream", as in a
mental image, generated by imagination and memory, which was able to clarify
reality. Later, the Middle-earth Elves gave him the name "Mithrandir". He was also
called "Tharkûn" by the Dwarves, and "Gandalf" by the Men.
12. Tolkien, J.R.R. *The Silmarillion*. London: HarperCollins, 1999, p. 22.

Five wizards, named "Istari" by the Elves, were sent by the Valar to Middle-earth, to fight off the dark power that was taking over, when the Dark Lord was mustering forces to recover the One Ring. They were Curunír, known as Saruman; two Blue Wizards who went into the East and never returned; Radagast, the Brown, who took great interest for plants and animals; and Gandalf, the Grey, who kept faithful to his mission of aiding the Children of Ilúvatar. The Wizards took on physical shapes, generally embodied as elderly people. "The archetype of the Old Wise Man is fundamentally the human being's ability to glimpse that which religions call a manifestation of deity, through his authority, power and wisdom".[13]

Gandalf plays the role of the fatherly figure, now close to the other members of the Fellowship, helping and guiding them, then disappearing unexpectedly, letting them grow and walk on their own — reappearing in unusual ways, making them sure that they are never alone.

> In traditional narratives, such as folktales, the role of parents is mostly that of dispatchers and occasionally donors. The dispatcher role means that the parents either directly send the child away from home into the dangerous world (*Little Red Riding Hood*; *Hansel and Gretel*) or by their absence, often death, expose the child to dangers (*Cinderella*). The parents thus presented cannot be evaluated psychologically, as "bad" or "evil," since they necessarily must have this particular function in the narrative. Sometimes the absent parent may act as a guardian and donor. [...] Again, we cannot judge this figure as "good" but merely state that her role in the story is providing the protagonist with magical agents (donor).[14]

Having Nikolajeva's considerations in mind, we can say that Gandalf acts as a dispatcher, disturbing the peaceful life of the Hobbits, pushing them away from their comfort zone and,

---

13. Klautau, D. G. 'Do Cinzento ao Branco: o processo de individuação a partir de Gandalf em *O Senhor dos Anéis*'. *Ciberteologia: Revista de Teologia & Cultura*, 10, 2007, pp. 10-12.

14. Nikolajeva, M. *The Rhetoric of Character in Children's Literature*. Lanham, Maryland: The Scarecrow Press, 2003, p. 117.

apparently, bringing them trouble. But we know that Gandalf is far from representing an evil to the Hobbits. On the contrary, he is the only one who turns his eyes to the huge value of the Halflings, and he knows that the greatest power against the evil forces in Middle-earth comes from the Shire. At the same time, the Istar is a donor, because his presence is beneficial to the free peoples of Middle-earth.

In a letter, Tolkien explains Gandalf's physical form and his role in the saga:

> At this point in the fabulous history the purpose was precisely to limit and hinder their exhibition of 'power' on the physical plane, and so that they should do what they were primarily sent for: train, advise, instruct, arouse the hearts and minds of those threatened by Sauron to a resistance with their own strengths; and not just to do the job for them.[15]

Divine providence, represented by the Valar's determinations, in Valinor, and by the presence of the Istari in Middle-earth, was there to prevent the free peoples from being forsaken in face of Sauron's threats. At the same time, their greatest contribution was, like the divine grace, to "train, advise, instruct, arouse the hearts and minds of those threatened by Sauron to a resistance with their own strengths; and not just to do the job for them". Such training demanded a response from the individuals whom Gandalf helped. Thus, the wizard encouraged the heroes to practice virtue, so necessary for their individual, relational, communal, and political growth.

It was from Nienna, Lady of Tears, that Olórin received precious gifts, indispensable for the acquisition of virtue, which is, in turn, essential for happiness and for the happy ending of Tolkien's story. With Nienna, Gandalf learned values such as compassion, patience, and hope. Above all, he learned mercy, a *sine qua non* condition for the victory of the free peoples against the power of the Ring.

---

15. Tolkien, J.R.R., Carpenter, H. (Org.), Tolkien, C. (Assist.). *The Letters of J.R.R. Tolkien*. Op. cit., Letter 156, p. 202.

Nienna is one of the Queens of the Valar, counted among the eight most powerful ones, called the "Aratar". It is said that in the Ainulindalë, the Music of the Ainur, her part was the one most laden with grief and, with her, suffering entered the world from the beginning. In a hasty interpretation, one could see her as a negative Ainu, just like Melkor, because suffering is not well-regarded. However, it is not said that Nienna brought evil, she only took pity of it. The suffering she brought, then, is not evil itself, it is an acknowledgment and a reparation of it.

Nienna dwells alone, and she is the sister of the Fëanturi, the Masters of Spirits, whose powers are more related to the metaphysical plane, different from the other Valar. The suffering that entered the world through her music was linked to the idea of sacrifice, of looking outside one's self, of taking pity on someone else's pain: characteristics which are exclusive to those who love. It is said in *The Silmarillion*:

> She is acquainted with grief, and mourns for every wound that Arda has suffered in the marring of Melkor. So great was her sorrow, as the Music unfolded, that her song turned to lamentation long before its end, and the sound of mourning was woven into the themes of the World before it began. *But she does not weep for herself; and those who hearken to her learn pity, and endurance in hope.*[16]

Tolkien was a great supporter of Western civilization and would often place in the west everything that he considered positive. The fact that Nienna lived "west of West" means that her benign force was even more accentuated. Her powers were ahead of the disgraces that were still to happen.

The Valië is a powerful model of something that goes beyond compassion: mercy, showing pity even for Melkor, the most powerful and the cruelest of the Ainur, who chose to rebel against Eru. Thus, Nienna's wisdom was passed on to Olórin, i.e., the Wizard Gandalf, and we can infer that the most important of the Istar's missions was, in large measure, transmitted by her intercession.

---

16. Tolkien, J.R.R. *The Silmarillion*. Op. cit., p. 19. Emphasis added.

In *The Hobbit*, the presence of compassion as a virtue plays an important role, influencing the outcome of the adventures in *The Lord of the Rings*. In the chapter "Riddles in the Dark", when Bilbo uses the Ring to escape from Gollum, after winning the riddle contest, he finds the opportunity to kill the strange creature, but does not do it:

> Bilbo [...] was desperate. [...] He must fight. He must stab the foul thing, put its eyes out, kill it. It meant to kill him. *No, not a fair fight. He was invisible now.* Gollum had no sword. Gollum had not actually threatened to kill him, or tried to yet. And he was miserable, alone, lost. *A sudden understanding, a pity mixed with horror, welled up in Bilbo's heart.*[17]

We can notice the presence of Nienna in this "sudden understanding, a pity mixed with horror" that "welled up in Bilbo's heart", even though the text itself does not give us concrete elements. However, when we go back to the dialogue Frodo had with Gandalf in the Shire, 77 years after the struggle between Bilbo and Gollum, in the chapter "The Shadow of the Past" of *The Lord of the Rings*, we see more clearly the issue of mercy as a determining factor in the fate of the Ring, associated to the event described in *The Hobbit*.

> 'What a pity that Bilbo did not stab that vile creature, when he had a chance!'
> '*Pity? It was Pity that stayed his hand. Pity, and Mercy*: not to strike without need [...]'
> 'I am sorry,' said Frodo. 'But I am frightened; and I do not feel any pity for Gollum. [...] He deserves death.'
> 'Deserves it! I daresay he does. Many that live deserve death. And some that die deserve life. Can you give it to them? *Then do not be too eager to deal out death in judgement. For even the very wise cannot see all ends.*'[18]

---

17. Tolkien, J.R.R. *The Hobbit*. London: HarperCollins, 2006, pp. 101-102. Emphasis added.
18. Tolkien, J.R.R. *The Lord of the Rings*. Op. cit., p. 78. Emphasis added.

Having in mind the years of experience Gandalf (Olórin) had as an apprentice of Nienna's, the hypothesis of the Valië's influence on her pupil's wisdom becomes plausible — a determining factor for the success of the Quest. We know that Frodo recalls that dialogue when he and Sam find Gollum and tame him. Frodo, thus, conquers the temptation of harming Gollum, different from what Sam considered the right thing to do. Frodo, by mercy, prefers to trust Gollum, even being aware of his ill intentions.

Thomas Aquinas reminds that mercy is the compassion for someone else's misery:

> from the very fact that a person takes pity on anyone, it follows that another's distress grieves him. And since sorrow or grief is about one's own ills, one grieves or sorrows for another's distress, in so far as one looks upon another's distress as one's own.[19]

We cannot exactly say that Frodo feels mercy towards Gollum in the first way, by which "one who loves considers his friend his own self". One would expect it from Nienna or, on a deeper level, from Eru Himself — the One, sovereign God — because they are pure spirits, untainted by Evil. But he does feel the second way, inasmuch as he believes he could suffer from similar grief by seeing in Gollum something he could become, knowing how much evil the Ring caused to him during the years he had the object. It was painful for Frodo to carry it.

Sam, even though he was not a pure spirit, by self-forgetfulness, keeping the proportions, could be included in the first meaning of mercy in relation to his master — but not to Gollum. He shares Frodo's pains as though they were his own and because of that he does not feel angry when his master relapses. He recognises in his friend all the pain he feels; he is compassionate and forgiving. But the gardener is also a flawed individual and, therefore, he is merciful towards Frodo in the

---

19. Aquinas, T. *The Summa Theologica*. Translated by the Fathers of the English Dominican province. London: Catholic Way Publishing, 2014,. SS, Q30, A2.

second way: by knowing that the evil the Ring causes to Frodo could happen to himself and the other free peoples of Middle-earth.[20]

Thomas Aquinas discusses the grandiosity of mercy among virtues:

> Hence mercy is accounted as being proper to God: and therein His omnipotence is declared to be chiefly manifested.
> [...]. But of all the virtues which relate to our neighbour, mercy is the greatest, even as its act surpasses all others, since it belongs to one who is higher and better to supply the defect of another, in so far as the latter is deficient.[21]

Our hypothesis is that virtue is the supreme good of Men, and that it is responsible for bringing about the happy ending of the War of the Ring. Frodo, even though he succumbed to the Ring, conquered the greatest of virtues among his peers.

Tolkien discusses the Hobbit's mission in one of his letters:

> I do not think that Frodo's was a *moral* failure. At the last moment the pressure of the Ring would reach its maximum – impossible, I should have said, for any one to resist [...] Frodo had done what he could and spent himself completely (as an instrument of Providence) and had produced a situation in which the object of his quest could be achieved. His humility (with which he began) and his sufferings were justly rewarded by the highest honour; and his exercise of patience and mercy towards Gollum gained him Mercy: his failure was redressed.[22]

Frodo, therefore, is not a failure, but a hero: not because he achieved something that was above his strengths, but because he nourished within him compassion and mercy towards the other. This was enough for the success of his mission.

Even though Gollum did not want to become definitively

---

20. He understands Frodo even more by bearing the Ring for some hours in Cirith Ungol, when he thought Frodo had been killed by Shelob.
21. Aquinas, T. *The Summa Theologica*. op. cit., SS, Q30, A4.
22. Tolkien, J.R.R., Carpenter, H. (Org.), Tolkien, C. (Assist.). *The Letters of J.R.R. Tolkien*. Op. cit., Letter 246, p. 326.

evil towards his master, his willpower was extremely fragile
and his attachment to the Ring was stronger than his weak
attempts to abandon his new identity. What particularly attracts
attention is the self-destructive characteristic of Evil: more
than the opposition from those who choose virtue, the very
denial of good — evil — is responsible for its own failure.

Tolkien's characters always have light and shadow within
them, and what is evil is thus characterised by the results of its
choices. The Professor discusses that in a letter:

> In my story I do not deal in Absolute Evil. I do not think there is
> such a thing, since that is Zero. I do not think that at any rate any
> 'rational being' is wholly evil. Satan fell. In my myth Morgoth fell
> before Creation of the physical world. In my story Sauron represents
> as near an approach to the wholly evil will as is possible.[23]

Gandalf, the Wizard, probably learned this truth from
Nienna, that all Ilúvatar's creatures, as such, have the essential
possibility of living in virtue, finding the chief good, happiness.
That is why mercy, in its most sublime form, exerted by means
of forgiveness, is encouraged by the Istar. Gandalf, through
this lesson, wants to show the greatest of all weapons against
evil: reconciliation, by means of self-knowledge and the
acknowledgement of one's own mistakes; and trust, based on
hope, that one can choose a different path.

When Gandalf challenges Saruman in Isengard, he does not
want to destroy him. On the contrary, he gives Saruman the
chance to repent and change his behaviour. Thus, the wizard
does not teach solely with words, but also through example, by
the most sublime way of exerting mercy: through the practice
of forgiveness. 'I do not wish to kill you, or hurt you, as you
would know, if you really understood me. And I have the
power to protect you. I am giving you a last chance. You can
leave Orthanc, free – if you choose.'[24]

23. Id., Letter 183, p. 243.
24. Tolkien, J.R.R. *The Lord of the Rings*. Op. cit., p. 760.

However, to achieve Gandalf's forgiveness, Saruman had to suffer one penalty: to relinquish temporarily his position in the Order of the Istari. Saruman would have to give up his objects, the key to the tower and his staff, as a proof of repentance and humbleness. The traitorous Istar, however, did not suffer humiliation and, on the contrary, chose mockery and hatred. When Saruman decides to turn his back to Gandalf, the latter passes sentence and expels Saruman from the Order and the Council, locking him in the tower of Orthanc, invigilated by the Ents.

> At last, with Saruman's madness and Gandalf's gesture of mercy, the White Rider assumes his position in the order of the Istari and in the White Council. He is the master of tradition, the light of the Valar and of Ilúvatar, the One. Symbolically, Gandalf, the White, expresses, at this moment, the social function of the *Self*, who affirms the identity of the group, discerns the elements that interfere in the process of individuation, and imposes the truth, the justice, and the responsibility before challenges.[25]

From gardener to master

When Sam and Frodo are in Minas Morgul, climbing the stairs of Cirith Ungol to reach the fires of Mount Doom, following Gollum's suggestion, the Hobbits have a dialogue which reveals the plot itself, their roles in that story, and the meaning of their quest. Sam says:

> '[...] The brave things in the old tales and songs, Mr. Frodo: adventures, as I used to call them. I used to think that they were things the wonderful folk of the stories went out and looked for, because they wanted them [...]. But that's not the way of it with the tales that really mattered, or the ones that stay in the mind. Folk seem to have been just landed in them, usually – their paths were laid that way, as you put it. But I expect they had lots of chances, like us, of turning back, only they didn't. And if they had,

25. Klautau, D. G. 'Do Cinzento ao Branco: o processo de individuação a partir de Gandalf em O Senhor dos Anéis'. Ciberteologia: Revista de Teologia & Cultura, n.10, 2007, pp. 9-10.

we shouldn't know, because they'd have been forgotten. We hear about those as just went on – and not all to a good end, mind you; at least not to what folk inside a story and not outside it call a good end. You know, coming home, and finding things all right, though not quite the same – like old Mr. Bilbo. [...]'[26]

Sam's speech reveals much of his personality and how the character was developed throughout the story. We know he is a rustic young hobbit, who had just come of age,[27] a gardener, the son of Hamfast Gamgee, both of them Bilbo and Frodo's employees. Sam is also an idealist and fascinated by stories of Elves, dragons, and everything that sparked magic from beyond the Shire. Because the Hobbits lived somewhat remotely from the rest of Middle-earth, their lives were closer to ours: trivial, ordinary, concrete. Leaving the Shire meant, thus, leaving the Primary World (that is, from an inside-the-story perspective, which to us corresponds to the Secondary World) and entering the world of fantasy (which is not mere fantasy in the context of the story, but a distant reality for the Hobbits).

We learn more about Samwise Gamgee in the first chapter, "A Long-expected Party", when he is mentioned by his father in a conversation among Hobbits, about Bilbo's adventures and the world beyond the Shire:

'[…] my lad Sam will know more about that. He's in and out of Bag End. Crazy about stories of the old days, he is, and he listens to all Mr. Bilbo's tales. Mr. Bilbo has learned him his letters – meaning no harm, mark you, and I hope no harm will come of it.
   'Elves and Dragons! I says to him. *Cabbages and potatoes are better for me and you. Don't go getting mixed up in the business of your betters, or you'll land in trouble too big for you,* I says to him. […]'[28]

By saying that, Hamfast Gamgee, the Gaffer, shows that Sam bears two worlds within him: that of a rustic young hobbit,

---

26. Tolkien, J.R.R. *The Lord of the Rings*. Op. cit., pp. 931-932.
27. Sam was 35 when he departed from the Shire with Frodo. A Hobbit comes of age at 33.
28. Tolkien, J.R.R. *The Lord of the Rings*. Op. cit., p. 31.

with his manual work and simple speech, who desires, at the same time, to know the world out of his house, with the wise and the brave, its great deeds and erudition. In the following chapter, "The Shadow of the Past", the gardener makes his first appearance:

> 'Queer things you do hear these days, to be sure,' said Sam.
> 'Ah,' said Ted, 'you do, if you listen. But I can hear fireside-tales and children's stories at home, if I want to.'
> '[…] I've heard tell that Elves are moving west. They do say they are going to the harbours, out away beyond the White Towers.' […]
> 'Well, that isn't anything new, if you believe the old tales. And I don't see what it matters to me or you. Let them sail! But I warrant you haven't seen them doing it; nor anyone else in the Shire.'
> '[…] There's Mr. Baggins now, that I work for. He told me that they were sailing and he knows a bit about Elves. And old Mr. Bilbo knew more: many's the talk I had with him when I was a little lad.'
> 'Oh, they're both cracked,' said Ted. 'Leastways old Bilbo was cracked, and Frodo's cracking. […]
> Sam sat silent and said no more. […] But Sam had more on his mind than gardening.[29]

The seemingly unpretentious conversation between Sam and Ted Sandyman — who had the other Hobbits in his favour — has some meaningful subtleties. The character, moreover, refers to concepts that Tolkien himself defended. When Ted says "But I can hear fireside-tales and children's stories at home, if I want to", Sam answers: "I daresay there's more truth in some of them than you reckon". Gamgee's claim refers to Tolkien's essay *On Fairy-stories*, already mentioned here, and also the author's concept about mythology. For Tolkien, fairy-stories are not mere childish distractions, but they reveal the profound understanding of men and the world, which traverse the fabric of our imagination.

Sam is as rustic as Ted and the other Hobbits, but his heart had experienced contact with a world beyond his rustic and concrete reality: he learned the fairy-stories from Bilbo, as

---

29. Tolkien, J.R.R. *The Lord of the Rings*. Op. cit., pp. 58-60.

a child, and could never forget what he learned about these realities outside his everyday life. Contrary to common belief, leaving home to look for Elves meant, for Sam, precisely abandoning his peaceful and childish universe and searching his personal growth.

Bilbo and Frodo were, more than his masters, people who inspired Sam, because they brought accounts and lessons from a world outside his daily one, a world he longed to know and experience. That is why it did not cost Sam much to follow Frodo out of the Shire, since Baggins was, for him, worthy of great admiration and a person who enabled him to make his seemingly childish dreams come true. Gamgee could not anticipate the imminent peril but saw in the comings and goings of Elves and Dwarves through the Shire a world of possibilities.

Sam did not know that the desire nourished in his heart was, in fact, something beyond his volition, a mission, a calling or vocation, in the religious sense. "Folk seem to have been just landed in them, usually – their paths were laid that way",[30] he told Frodo on the stairs of Cirith Ungol. The gardener responded to this calling by answering only to what was most important in his heart — the fascination for adventures and the immense admiration he had for Bilbo and, especially, Frodo.

Tolkien writes a little on the development of the character Samwise Gamgee in a letter to the reader Mrs. Eileen Elgar:

> Sam is meant to be lovable and laughable. Some readers he irritates and even infuriates. I can well understand it. [...] He is a more representative hobbit than any others that we have to see much of; and he has consequently a stronger ingredient of that quality which even some hobbits found at times hard to bear: a vulgarity — by which I do not mean a mere 'down-toearthiness' — a mental myopia which is proud of itself, a smugness (in varying degrees) and cocksureness, and a readiness to measure and sum up all things from a limited experience, largely enshrined in sententious traditional 'wisdom'.[31]

---

30. Id., p. 931.
31. Tolkien, J.R.R., Carpenter, H. (Org.), Tolkien, C. (Assist.). *The Letters of J.R.R. Tolkien*. Op. cit., Letter 246, p. 329.

Gamgee did not know, but saying "yes" to that adventure would entail the most important achievement of his personal growth, the romantic character goes from a simple young dreamer, even provincial, to a man sure of himself, capable of making deliberate decisions and playing a prominent role in the story. The countryside gardener proves to be not only a faithful companion to Frodo — which would be enough for a study on friendship — but also a rich and deep individual that Edward Morgan Foster would categorise as a "round character":

> The test of a round character is whether it is capable of surprising in a convincing way. If it never surprises, it is flat. If it does not convince, it is a flat pretending to be round. It has the incalculability of life about it — life within the pages of a book.[32]

It is more common — maybe even easier — to build round characters that surprise the reader by not following the path of virtue, but of vice, as it happens in the Primary World. The saga of the Ring, however, presents characters that surprise by means of virtue, an even greater challenge for those who, already in the beginning of the story, are relatively virtuous, such as Sam — or, at least, more innocent than harmful — but who develop into higher levels of excellence, towards perfection — even though they can never reach it, since they are not gods, but fallible, limited beings. In the Aristotelian philosophical conception, they move towards the chief good (*eudaimonia*); in Christian doctrine, that is sanctity, the eternal communion with God.

> Aristotle, in his *Nicomachean Ethics*, claims that "moral virtue is moderation or observance of the mean, and in what sense, viz, as holding a middle position between two vices, one on the side of excess, and the other on the side of deficiency, and as aiming at the mean or moderate amount both in feeling and in action".[33]

The mean, however, is not an exactly calculated measure, but a sensible one, sometimes moving more towards excess

32. Forster, E.M. *Aspects of the Novel*. New York: RosettaBooks, 2002, p. 55.
33. Aristotle. *The Nicomachean Ethics*. Op. cit., p. 55.

than deficiency and vice-versa, because the mean is "not the absolute but the relative mean.".[34] Likewise, "not all actions nor all passions that admit of moderation; there are some whose very name imply badness".[35] The philosopher also categorises virtues in "moral" and "intellectual", saying that the latter "owes its birth and growth mainly to instruction, and so requires time and experience, while moral excellence is the result of habit or custom [...]".[36]

Sam is a simple Hobbit, whose work is manual but, as his father suggests, he learned his letters from Bilbo, who also taught him the stories of Elves. He certainly was not as educated as Frodo was, but he learned from his masters because he was interested in the universe beyond the Shire and, therefore, he knows about the stories of the ancient peoples of Middle-earth.

But the kind of virtue that calls our attention to Sam, and that is developed throughout the story, is not exactly intellectual, but moral. Sam develops his courage, generosity, and self-control along the way from the Shire to Mordor. His main characteristic is, from the beginning, faithfulness: he does not want to abandon Frodo Baggins, whom he calls "master". His faithfulness collaborated for his personal growth and prevented him from straying from his destined course. Therefore, he paradoxically achieved independence as an award for not sticking to him whom he served and loved.

Sam, however, would not be able to complete the hero's journey had he not, from the beginning, been acting freely and aiming at goodness, since virtues in general are

Forms of moderation or modes of observing the mean, and that they are habits or trained faculties, and that they show themselves in the performance of the same acts which produce them, and that they depend on ourselves and are voluntary, and that they follow the guidance of right reason.[37]

34. Id., p. 45.
35. Id., p. 47.
36. Id., p. 34.
37. Id., p. 79.

Among other things, Sam feels anger, indignation, fear, enthusiasm, and joy, as do all minimally credible characters in fiction, considering what we are in the Primary World. But his outlook in relation to these passions gradually turns towards goodness, because he does not lose sight of his primary mission: to serve Frodo and collaborate for the Quest to be fulfilled.

In his letter to Mrs. Eileen Elgar, Tolkien goes on:

> Sam was cocksure, and deep down a little conceited; but his conceit had been transformed by his devotion to Frodo. He did not think of himself as heroic or even brave, or in any way admirable – except in his service and loyalty to his master. That had an ingredient (probably inevitable) of pride and possessiveness: it is difficult to exclude it from the devotion of those who perform such service.[38]

Sam's relationship with Frodo is similar to a batman and his superior officer in a war. John Garth, author of *Tolkien and the Great War*, one of the most notable of Tolkien's biographies, wrote in his internet article "Sam Gamgee and Tolkien's batmen" that, apart from his vast knowledge on mythological and medieval matters, his life should be highlighted, and that his experience in the First World War informed much of the construction of his characters, including the faithful Samwise.

Garth presents a letter from Tolkien to a reader, Humphrey Cotton Minchin, written in 1956, which corroborates his claim:

> My 'Samwise' is indeed (as you note) largely a reflexion of the English soldier – grafted on the village-boys of early days, the memory of the privates and my batmen that I knew in the 1914 War, and recognized as so far superior to myself.[39]

---

38. Tolkien, J.R.R., Carpenter, H. (Org.), Tolkien, C. (Assist.). *The Letters of J.R.R. Tolkien*. Op. cit., Letter 246, p. 329.
39. Garth, John. 'Sam Gamgee and Tolkien's Batmen', <https://johngarth.wordpress.com/2014/02/13/sam-gamgee-and-tolkiens-batmen/> [Accessed 28 May 2020].

The biographer calls attention to the fact that Tolkien called the batmen "my batmen": one understands, then, that Tolkien himself had his batmen — not all at once, but different ones at different moments. Garth reminds, however, that such a relationship was not typical of the Professor's personality, mentioning a letter he wrote to his son Christopher Tolkien: "the most improper job of any man [...] is bossing other men. Not one in a million is fit for it, and least of all those who seek the opportunity".[40]

Still in his article, quoting a paper on Tolkien he had delivered at Marquette University in 2004, Garth reinforces that the relationship between both Hobbits reflects that between an officer and his servant during the First World War.

Officers had a university education and a middle-class background. Working-class men stayed at the rank of private or at best sergeant. A social gulf divides the literate, leisured Frodo from his former gardener, now responsible for wake-up calls, cooking and packing.[41]

Such is the initial relationship between the two Hobbits, but it changes throughout the journey. Frodo, however, never treats Sam arrogantly: his demeanour is always welcoming and equal. The servant relationship is emphasised by Sam's behaviour, who never thinks of stopping serving Frodo, and who does not see himself as a hero,[42] as Tolkien wrote in his letter.

Kept in proportion, Sam plays the role of Sancho Panza in relation to Frodo. It is not possible to say that Frodo has the idealistic traits of Don Quixote, but the power of the Ring sometimes, especially at the end of the Quest, puts Frodo in a kind of mental trance. Sam, in turn, always brings him back to his true mission. Even though he is a dreaming lad, it is Sam who keeps Frodo's feet firmly grounded against the power of the Ring.

40. Ibid.
41. Ibid.
42. Except for a moment when he bears the Ring in the tower of Cirith Ungol.

As Sancho Panza, Gamgee is inseparable from Frodo, and it is his fidelity that edifies him in the Saga. When Sam is chosen to follow Frodo in the journey to Rivendell, or even after the Council of Elrond, to follow the appointed Ring-bearer, it can be said that Sam attained these positions by mere luck. In the first instance, still in the Shire, he was eavesdropping the conversation between Gandalf and Frodo, and learned what was happening and what should be done from then on. Because he was discovered, it was decided that he would go with Frodo to the Last Homely House. Something similar happened during the Council of Elrond because Sam clandestinely took part in the meeting. When Elrond learned that Sam had heard it all, he designated the gardener to accompany Frodo in the grievous journey to Mount Doom.

In the chapter "The Breaking of the Fellowship", we see Sam's heart closer to Frodo, and his journey besides Bilbo's heir is no longer due to chance but down to their strong bonds. When the members of the Society realised that Frodo had disappeared, they soon split to look for him, under Aragorn's orders. Sam, however, lagged behind and was left alone.

> 'Something scared Mr. Frodo badly. He screwed himself up to the point, sudden. He made up his mind at last – to go. Where to? Off East. Not without Sam? Yes, without even his Sam. That's hard, cruel hard. [...] Back to the boats, Sam, like lightning!'
> [...] 'Coming, Mr. Frodo! Coming!' called Sam, and flung himself from the bank, clutching at the departing boat. He missed it by a yard. With a cry and a splash he fell face downward into deep swift water. [...]
> An exclamation of dismay came from the empty boat. A paddle swirled and the boat put about. [...]
> 'Up you come, Sam my lad!' said Frodo. 'Now take my hand!'
> 'Save me, Mr. Frodo!' gasped Sam. 'I'm drowned. I can't see your hand.'
> [...] Frodo brought the boat back to the bank, and Sam was able to scramble out, wet as a water-rat.
> [...] 'So all my plan is spoilt!' said Frodo. 'It is no good trying to escape you. But I'm glad, Sam. I cannot tell you how glad.'[43]

43. Tolkien, J.R.R. *The Lord of the Rings*. Op. cit., pp. 528-530.

Sam's legs are short, he is not as tall as Strider, and he cannot reach him to look for Frodo. Still, he has got an advantage in relation to the future king: his heart and mind are connected to Frodo. The gardener knows his physical limitations, but the love for his friend makes him use his head. Through reasoning and the affinity with Baggins, he manages to find out where his master was and his plans.

Sam's will to follow Frodo is almost unmeasurable: he risks his own life, almost drowning in the river before a seemingly empty boat, but he correctly suspects it is his master escaping with the invisibility ring. Frodo reacts as if surprised, but also relieved: Bilbo's heir does not want to be alone, and he knows that Sam is the best company in his long and burdensome journey.

From this moment, the friendship between the Hobbits grows stronger, and the hierarchical difference between them starts to diminish. This situation, similar to that of two soldiers in a war, makes room for the practice of courage as a virtue, which collaborates for each one's personal development, and it grows in strength and meaning — both of them are spurred by a cause, but they are also valiant enough to save one another.

According to Aristotle, the citizen-soldier's courage is the closest to true courage, even more so if it is practiced out of free will, as in the Hobbits' case and the whole Fellowship members', since "a man ought to be courageous, not under compulsion, but because it is noble to be so".[44] The philosopher claims that courageous people are more intense in moments of danger but, in general, they are peaceful. Besides, the person "He, then, that endures and fears what he ought from the right motive, and in the right manner, and at the right time, and similarly Peels confidence, is courageous".[45]

---

44. Aristotle. *The Nicomachean Ethics*. Op. cit., p. 86.
45. Id., p. 83.

Choices lead to decisions

Sam has his crucial opportunity to show his bravery when he is faced with the fearsome giant spider Shelob, when he returns from a fight with Gollum that prevents him from defending Frodo from that enemy. According to Aristotle, "by habituating ourselves to despise danger, and to face it, we become courageous; and when we have become courageous, we are best able to face danger."[46] Sam, along with Frodo, had already been to many terrible places: they crossed the Barrow-downs; escaped from the Nazgûl; continued their journey, in spite of losing Gandalf in Moria; crossed the Dead Marshes, among other perils, before facing the terrifying Shelob.

The ordeals Sam had faced strengthened his character, and at that moment he had enough courage to face the malignant spider. When he found his master on the floor, being dragged by Shelob, he charged. Sam did not have enough time to think; he acted as he had been acting until then. At that moment, he was strong enough to face a creature which no one dared to face, not even Sauron himself. He needed some external artifices beyond his own strength, and he counted on luck — or divine providence — to beat her, but this would not have taken place if Sam had been a coward before her.

The artifices he used were the tools that helped him against Shelob, such as Frodo's elven sword, Sting, apart from the Phial of Galadriel, the parting gift given to Frodo by the Elf when the departed from Lothlórien.

> [...] cold and hard and solid it seemed to his touch in a phantom world of horror, the Phial of Galadriel. [...]
> As if his indomitable spirit had set its potency in motion, the glass blazed suddenly like a white torch in his hand. [...] The beams of it entered into her wounded head and scored it with unbearable pain, and the dreadful infection of light spread from eye to eye. She fell back beating the air with her forelegs, her sight blasted by inner lightnings, her mind in agony.[47]

---

46. Aristotle. *The Nicomachean Ethics*. Op. cit., p. 38.
47. Tolkien, J.R.R. *The Lord of the Rings*. Op. cit., pp. 954-955.

Sam, as though praying, calls on Galadriel and Elbereth, Queen of the Valar, by means of a hymn to Elbereth, using the Phial of Galadriel which contained the light of Eärendil, the blessed Elf of past ages. The invocation to Galadriel-Elbereth makes up for the presence of the mother, in the supernatural plane, as Mary for the Catholics. The motherly love aids the Hobbit, helping him in his moment of despair, but the strength of the "son" is not to be disregarded.

The Hobbit manages, at last, to beat Shelob definitively when she falls upon the elven blade he was holding. The terrible spider is defeated due to her own weight and the courage and persistence of an infinitely weaker creature. Completely enfeebled, she retreats, never to return in that story.

After that, Sam's courage is more subtly tested. His bravery suffers a still greater pain: after defeating the giant spider, he finds his friend lying still, bound in cords contrived by Shelob, and he deems him dead. Baggins's apparent death means, in a way, Sam's own death: "'All alone and without me to help you? I couldn't have a borne it, it'd have been the death of me'",[48] said Gamgee when he learned that Frodo wanted to leave the whole Fellowship behind after Boromir's attack.

The Gaffer's son felt abandoned but, at the same time, because of the long journey he had undertaken, he already had all the necessary qualities to make independent decisions. This was the first significant severance between them; the second happened in the end, when Frodo went to the Undying Lands with Bilbo, Gandalf, and the Elves, while Gamgee went back home to stay with his family.

Sam could hardly believe his master was dead: his first reaction was to check if he was indeed lifeless. Frodo was still, pale, would not speak, his heart did not beat, and his breath could not be felt: "'Often he chafed his master's hands and feet, and touched his brow, but all were cold.'"[49] At last, Gamgee gave in: his master was gone.

48. Id., p. 530.
49. Id., p. 955.

After crying copiously, Sam decides to follow on, and well-equipped: he takes the sword, the mithril coat Frodo had been given by Bilbo, and the Phial of Galadriel. But, to fulfil the Quest, he must take the most important object: Sauron's Ring itself.

'What? *Me* take the Ring from *him*? The Council gave it to him.' But the answer came at once: 'And the Council gave him companions, so that the errand should not fail. And you are the last of all the Company. The errand must not fail.' [...]
    'Let me see now: if we're found here, or Mr. Frodo's found, and that Thing's on him, well, the Enemy will get it. And that's the end of all of us, of Lórien, and Rivendell, and the Shire and all. [...] He drew a deep breath. 'Then take It, it is!'[50]

The way Sam refers to the Ring demands our attention. He calls it "Thing", which sets a drastic opposition with Gollum, who calls it "Precious". While Gamgee considers Isildur's Bane something contemptible, not worthy of having a name, Gollum is overly attached to it, considering it a treasure. Therefore, the effect of the Ring over the humble Sam was less strong than it was in Sméagol, who kills his friends in a few minutes, coveting the malignant ring.

As it happened with Gollum, Sam has internal dialogues, full of doubt, fear, anxiety, and he seems to talk to his own conscience, giving the impression that he heard some advice from supernatural beings who whispered good thoughts into his mind: "But the answer came at once: "And the Council gave him companions, so that the errand should not fail. And you are the last of all the Company. The errand must not fail."[51]

The Hobbit, however, did not stray from his mission. More than accompanying Frodo, he knew he had to defend an even greater good, for the Shire, Lórien, Rivendell, and the whole Middle-earth. Most of all, he knew that the noblest way to

---

50. Tolkien, J.R.R. *The Lord of the Rings*. Op. cit., pp. 957-958. Emphasis by the author.
51. Id., p. 957.

mourn his seemingly dead friend was to continue the Quest, even if alone. That is why he was not split in two, as Gollum was, and faced ordeals from this episode until the destruction of the Ring.

The fight between Sam and Shelob and the decision of taking the Ring after the presumed death of his friend are contained precisely in the chapter called "The Choices of Master Samwise". The title is interesting because Sam had never appeared as "master": it was Frodo who had always been thus named. Besides, we know that Gamgee's behaviour had always been servile, never one of leadership. The word "master", moreover, refers to a wise, knowledgeable, and experienced person, and even though Sam had attended some "classes" with Bilbo, he was a rustic young adult, with a less cultivated language and demeanour.

Because of everything he experiences throughout the journey, Sam grows in wisdom and metamorphoses from gardener into master. What gives him his new status is his decision-making skill: Sam is now a mature person who, because of his "choices" is called a "master".

> But now, having found that an act is involuntary when done under compulsion or through ignorance, we may conclude that a voluntary act is one which is originated by the doer with knowledge of the particular circumstances of the act.[52]

Sam's decision becomes ever more valuable, turning him into a master because he volunteers — not because he wants to serve his boss or because he wants to see the beings regarded as legendary in the Shire, but because he knows he has an obligation to all the free peoples of Middle-earth, to his friends, and his principles.

But voluntariness is not the only determining factor of Sam's choice. The philosopher deepens the concept of choice: "choice or purpose implies calculation and reasoning. The name itself,

---

52. Aristotle. *The Nicomachean Ethics.* Op. cit., p. 65.

too, seems to indicate this, implying that something is chosen before or in preference to other things."[53]

Indeed, it takes a long time for Sam to choose and, therefore, to make his decisions. Not because he wants to run away from obligation, but because he does not want to act on impulse — after all, when he understands that his friend is dead, he feels very angry at Gollum, who had contrived that trap in Shelob's lair for both Hobbits, but he knows that would not bring his friend back, nor would that be the most sensible thing to do, and not even because of a personal opinion. Sam tries to be reasonable, to tell right from wrong in regard to what he had set in the beginning of the journey.

The choices of Master Samwise are no guarantee that the Quest will have a happy ending. Sam tries to do what is in his power, even though he is small in the face of so many misfortunes. His smallness, however, enables him to go through unnoticed, and his humbleness is not a threat to the Ring, which has little power over him, when compared to the wise and the great.

> Since, then, a thing is said to be chosen or purposed when, being in our power, it is desired after deliberation, choice or purpose may be defined as deliberate desire for something in our power; for we first deliberate, and then, having made our decision thereupon, we desire in accordance with deliberation.[54]

Gamgee's choices were hard to make, but also had to be faced. When he finds out that his friend was not dead, but poisoned by Shelob, he tries to rescue him, but before that he had to go through the Orcs' obstacles and, even harder, through the consequences of carrying the burden of the Ring on his own:

> Already the Ring tempted him, gnawing at his will and reason. Wild fantasies arose in his mind; and he saw Samwise the Strong, Hero of the Age, striding with a flaming sword across the darkened

53. Aristotle. *The Nicomachean Ethics.* Op. cit., p. 68.
54. Id., p. 72.

land, and armies flocking to his call as he marched to the overthrow of Barad-dûr.[55]

The Quest, however, was not in Sam's hands: he is the Ring-bearer for a short period of time. It is Frodo who must return to complete the journey now that both are masters of themselves. The differences are undone, and they can be both called friends now.

The reunion with his friend is touching, but the proximity to Orodruin already shows its extremely strong effect on Frodo, who has barely any capacity of making his own choices. He needs Sam to go on, to the point of being carried by his own friend in Mount Doom.

> By then, the hierarchy is largely inverted. Frodo moves towards a childlike dependency: he presents the problems, Sam the solutions. In the First World War this process was far from atypical. Officers were given commissions for class reasons, not because they were experienced soldiers or leaders; whereas the privates and batmen often had the age, experience, and wisdom their official superiors lacked.[56]

Without Sam, Frodo would not have reached the end of his journey, would have been devoured by Shelob, attacked by the Orcs, or succumbed inside the Mountain. Gamgee saved him from such disasters and was there when the Ring was destroyed. The friend's company brought Frodo peace and ease amid the storm.

In their dialogue on the stairs of Cirith Ungol, before entering Shelob's lair, the Hobbits predict their future:

> '[...] Still, I wonder if we shall ever be put into songs or tales. [...] And people will say: "Let's hear about Frodo and the Ring!" And they'll say: "Yes, that's one of my favourite stories. Frodo was very brave, wasn't he, dad?" "Yes, my boy, the famousest of the hobbits, and that's saying a lot."'

---

55. Tolkien, J.R.R. *The Lord of the Rings.* Op. cit., p. 1178
56. Garth, John. 'Sam Gamgee and Tolkien's Batmen', Op. cit.

'It's saying a lot too much,' said Frodo, and he laughed, a long clear laugh from his heart. '[…] But you've left out one of the chief characters: Samwise the stouthearted. "I want to hear more about Sam, dad. Why didn't they put in more of his talk, dad? That's what I like, it makes me laugh. And Frodo wouldn't have got far without Sam, would he, dad?"'

'Now, Mr. Frodo,' said Sam, 'you shouldn't make fun. I was serious.'

'So was I,' said Frodo, 'and so I am.'[57]

Frodo's speech reveals his recognition of the gardener's condition as a hero: Sam's grandiosity in the saga is registered, therefore, in the very *Red Book* — Tolkien posed, as mentioned, as a mere translator of the story told by the Hobbits. In one of his letters, the author affirms that Sam Gamgee was not only grandiose, but in fact he was the main hero of the story, and his character was made not only of simple, rustic elements, but also of deeper and more elaborate ones. Sam displays the pragmatism of life connected to nature and, with it, he develops from the cultural and metaphysical point of view:

I think the simple 'rustic' love of Sam and his Rosie (nowhere elaborated) is absolutely essential to the study of his (the chief hero's) character, and to the theme of the relation of ordinary life (breathing, eating, working, begetting) and quests, sacrifice, causes, and the 'longing for Elves', and sheer beauty.[58]

In their farewell to Lothlórien, Galadriel gives to Sam Gamgee, as a parting gift, a box containing earth from Lórien, which the Hobbit used to restore much of the Shire that had been destroyed by Sharkey, the wizard Saruman, and his ruffians, after the destruction of the Ring. In the box, there was also a seed with a silver shale, which Sam planted and from which sprang "the only *mallorn* west of the Mountains and

57. Tolkien, J.R.R. *The Lord of the Rings*. Op. cit., pp. 932-933.
58. Tolkien, J.R.R., Carpenter, H. (Org.), Tolkien, C. (Assist.). *The Letters of J.R.R. Tolkien*. Op. cit., Letter 131, p. 161.

east of the Sea, and one of the finest in the world".[59]

Sam got married to Rosie Cotton, and they begot Elanor, who had an elven beauty. When she was only six months old, Frodo asked Sam to accompany him to Rivendell, where he would meet Bilbo, who was turning 131 years old. On that occasion, Frodo gives Sam the *Red Book of Westmarch*, which Bilbo had started, and Frodo continued: "'I have quite finished, Sam,' said Frodo. 'The last pages are for you.'"[60] Because Elanor was still very young, it was agreed that Sam would go only halfway, and then he would return to help Rosie.

But, instead of proceeding to Rivendell, they found the Elves and Bilbo on the way, and Sam realises that they are actually going to the Grey Havens, to the Undying Lands. This would be the greatest severance between them.

In the havens, they found the wizard Gandalf, who was also going to leave, and with him Merry and Pippin, who were there to accompany Sam on his way back home.

Sam had another twelve children with Rosie, he became mayor of the Shire seven times in a row, and only stopped when he was 96 years old. In the appendices to *The Lord of the Rings*, the end of his days is described:

> 1482 Death of Mistress Rose, wife of Master Samwise, on Mid-year's Day. On September 22 Master Samwise rides out from Bag End. He comes to the Tower Hills, and is last seen by Elanor, to whom he gives the Red Book afterwards kept by the Fairbairns. Among them the tradition is handed down from Elanor that Samwise passed the Towers, and went to the Grey Havens, and passed over Sea, last of the Ringbearers.[61]

The Undying Lands were a place to which only the Elves could go, with their ships, from Middle-earth. There lived the Valar, the Maiar, and the other Elves. Frodo, Bilbo, and, probably, Sam, were some of the rare exceptions of non-Elves

59. Tolkien, J.R.R. *The Lord of the Rings*. Op. cit., p. 1339.
60. Id., p. 1344.
61. Id., p. 1442.

who reached those lands, as a gift for having been Ring-bearers. They were to spend the rest of their days there, in the island of Tol Eressëa, resting and healing their wounds. "The passage over Sea is not Death. The 'mythology' is Elf-centred. According to it there was at first an actual Earthly Paradise, home and realm of the Valar, as a physical part of the earth."[62]

The master bequeaths his place

After having returned to the Shire and fought off Sharkey and his ruffians, the Hobbits had a season of peace, rebuilding the Shire, and prosperity. Frodo, however, felt weak and ill, because the wound in his shoulder caused by the leader of the Nazgûl on Weathertop, two years before, had not healed completely. Besides, everyone in the Shire talked about the great deeds of Merry, Pippin, and Sam, but as for Frodo, people did not remember him, something that afflicted master Gamgee.

Frodo, a noble, wise, and fair Hobbit, leaves the Shire voluntarily responding to a request made by his best friend, the wizard Gandalf. In Rivendell, already bearing a wound in his shoulder that would never heal, he understands his call and decides to volunteer to bear the Ring into the terrifying Mordor. He starves, he feels exhaustion, thirst, and pain. He loses his senses and much of his capacity for choice under the power of the Ring; he suffers the humiliation of succumbing at the very end of the journey. But Frodo is not the hero of the story. He brings within him all that a real-life human being in fact is; a being with flaws and doubts. According to Tolkien:

> [...] every event or situation has (at least) two aspects: the history and development of the individual [...], and the history of the world [...] — still there are abnormal situations in which one may be placed. 'Sacrificial' situations, I should call them: sc. positions

62. Tolkien, J.R.R., Carpenter, H. (Org.), Tolkien, C. (Assist.). *The Letters of J.R.R. Tolkien.* Op. cit., Letter 181, p. 237.

in which the 'good' of the world depends on the behaviour of an individual in circumstances which demand of him suffering and endurance far beyond the normal [...].
Frodo was in such a position [...]
The Quest was bound to fail as a piece of world-plan, and also was bound to end in disaster as the story of humble Frodo's development to the 'noble', his sanctification. Fail it would and did as far as Frodo considered alone was concerned.[63]

Bilbo's heir failed in the context of a romantic hero, for instance, but not if we consider what is feasible by an ordinary man, a contemporary man, closer to everyday life. His true battle was the interior one, the battle for virtue and, above all, love — and friendship is a kind of love (particularly if it is based on the notion of charity), and the most important one in the saga. For him to become a great hero, to reach sanctity, according to Tolkien, it was necessary for him to abandon his own self, giving his life for his friends[64] and not out of vanity.

But at this point the 'salvation' of the world and Frodo's own 'salvation' is achieved by his previous pity and forgiveness of injury. To 'pity' him [Gollum], to forbear to kill him, was a piece of folly, or a mystical belief in the ultimate value-in-itself of pity and generosity [...] By a situation created by his 'forgiveness', he was saved himself, and relieved of his burden.[65]

Baggins found salvation because he lived compassion in relation to Gollum, but he did not achieve his full purification. As a prize for his courage and voluntariness, he was granted permission to spend the rest of his days in Tol Eressëa, the Lonely Island, in the Undying Lands. Frodo could not receive the due praise for his deeds because his sanctification did not belong to Middle-earth anymore, but had a closer connection to the supernatural life, still material, but closer to the Valar:

63. Id., Letter 181, pp. 233-234.
64. See John 15:13: "Greater love hath no man than this, that a man lay down his life for his friends."
65. Tolkien, J.R.R., Carpenter, H. (Org.), Tolkien, C. (Assist.). *The Letters of J.R.R. Tolkien.* Op. cit., Letter 181, p. 234.

[...] it was not only nightmare memories of past horrors that afflicted him, but also unreasoning self-reproach: he saw himself and all that he done as a broken failure. [...] That was actually a temptation out of the Dark, a last flicker of pride [...]
Frodo was sent or allowed to pass over Sea to heal him [...]. So he went both to a purgatory and to a reward, for a while: a period of reflection and peace and a gaining of a truer understanding of his position in littleness and in greatness, spent still in Time amid the natural beauty of 'Arda Unmarred', the Earth unspoiled by evil.[66]

Frodo still feels his wounds because the action of the Ring indirectly left marks upon him, and this is especially due to the vestiges of his self-pride, for not accepting that he had failed and for his attachment to his own self; for not being able to give himself completely to the others — something he could not do, otherwise he would be God Himself. The Hobbit, however, is not a failure, but victorious. He gave everything his own weakness allowed and, therefore, he is noble and great. The fact that the people of the Shire forgot him is a grief not only to Sam, but to the reader too, who resents the probable "injustice" to Baggins in view of everything he did.

But such a neglect is opportune, because Frodo had to go through this ordeal to acknowledge his limitations, and to know that he had to give even more of himself. The Hobbit gets both punishment and consolation for his deeds: he would have time to purge his weaknesses and would find rest for his suffering in the Undying Lands, close to Bilbo.

In a 1944 letter to Christopher Tolkien, J.R.R. Tolkien's son and literary executor, ten years before the launching of *The Lord of the Rings* and five years before its completion, the Professor already had Frodo and Sam's ending in mind:

Sam is the most closely drawn character, the successor to Bilbo of the first book, the genuine hobbit. Frodo is not so interesting, because he has to be highminded, and has (as it were) a vocation.

---

66. Tolkien, J.R.R., Carpenter, H. (Org.), Tolkien, C. (Assist.). *The Letters of J.R.R. Tolkien.* Op. cit., Letter 246, pp. 327-328.

The book will prob. end up with Sam. Frodo will naturally become too ennobled and rarefied by the achievement of the great Quest, and will pass West with all the great figures; but S. will settle down to the Shire and gardens and inns.[67]

Tolkien uses a special word to describe Frodo: "highminded". The Hobbit is silent, reflexive, cautious, acts more than talks — the opposite of Sam — complains little, and often looks like someone who lacks brightness or strength. On the contrary, his personality is a result of an uncommon virtue of the average individual: high-mindedness. On this characteristic, Aristotle says:

> By a high-minded man we seem to moan one who claims much and deserves much [...]The high-minded man, then, in respect of the greatness of his deserts occupies an extreme position, but in that he behaves as he ought, observes the mean ; for he claims that which he deserves, while all the others claim too much or too little.[68]

While Tolkien claims that Samwise sometimes irritates the readers, Frodo is not described as irritating. He is always level-headed, with just a few excesses or faults and, therefore, his evolution as a character happens silently. He does not express his feelings and passions intensely, but he feels them all the same. He conceives and bends to his mission in a way that surprises even the wise. That is probably why Frodo had to be the Ring-bearer, as he was. He brought with him the humbleness of the Halflings and the greatness of the Wise. He was the one who could get the farthest, as he did, in the Quest.

> High-mindedness[69], then, seems to be the crowning grace, as it were, of the virtues; it makes them greater, and cannot exist without them. And on this account it is a hard thing to be truly high-minded; for it is impossible without the union of all the virtues.[70]

---

67. Id., Letter 93, p. 105.
68. Aristotle. *The Nicomachean Ethics*. Op. cit., p. 113.
69. In the sense of magnanimity, greatness of soul (μεγαλοψυχία).
70. Id., p. 115.

Frodo's high-mindedness, however, is not complete. It does not guarantee happiness, the chief good, because "the wise man will be happier than any one else".[71] Bilbo's heir would not reach a happy ending if he chose to fulfil his mission alone: he would not be high-minded, but simply haughty. He needed the help of his friends, such as Gandalf, the other members of the Fellowship and many other individuals among the free Men who won battles, eliminating the enemies, and deceiving *the* Enemy.

Frodo needed Bilbo's company too, the person he loved the most, in Tol Eressëa, because a Hobbit would hardly manage to be alone, without a peer. But the most important friendship he needed was Sam's. The gardener witnessed his failure in Mount Doom:

> [...] at the very Crack of Doom, stood Frodo, black against the glare, tense, erect, but still as if he had been turned to stone.
> 'Master!' cried Sam. [...]
> 'I have come,' he said. 'But I do not choose now to do what I came to do. I will not do this deed. The Ring is mine!' And suddenly, as he set it on his finger, he vanished from Sam's sight.[72]

The gardener, however, continued to love his master and considered him a friend, even though Frodo failed at the end of the Quest. Gamgee knew, more than anyone — because he knew his friend very well — that Frodo's mission was beyond his strength, and that his character was still good. "[...] when their [our friend's] reformation is possible, we are more bound to help them in their character than their fortune, inasmuch as character is a nobler thing, and has more to do with friendship than fortune has."[73]

With Sauron's downfall after the destruction of the Ring, Frodo and Sam got trapped in the volcanic fire of Mount Doom. Soon afterwards, Gandalf arrived with the Valinorean giant

---

71. Aristotle. *The Nicomachean Ethics*. Op. cit., p. 346.
72. Tolkien, J.R.R. *The Lord of the Rings*. Op. cit., p. 1237.
73. Aristotle. *The Nicomachean Ethics*. Op. cit., p. 293.

eagles Gwaihir, Landroval, and Meneldor, to rescue Frodo and Sam. Such an artifice shows the support of supernatural forces to the free peoples of Middle-earth.

The eagle's help is not exactly the use of a far-fetched resource, the *deus ex machina*, because the possibility of these birds intervening had always been present in the *legendarium* in the First, Second, and Third Ages. In the saga of the Ring itself, before rescuing the Hobbits from Mount Doom, the eagles had acted twice: in the first instance, they rescued Gandalf who had been trapped by Saruman on the pinnacle of Orthanc; in the second instance, they saved him from the peak of Celebdil, after Gandalf had defeated the Balrog. However, the eagles should be used sparingly in the story, as the author himself claims:

> The Eagles are a dangerous 'machine'. I have used them sparingly, and that is the absolute limit of their credibility or usefulness. The alighting of a Great Eagle of the Misty Mountains in the Shire is absurd; it also makes the later capture of G. by Saruman incredible, and spoils the account of his escape.[74]

The Eagles are governed by Manwë, Lord of the Airs and the Birds, and King of the Valar. Their presence in Middle-earth, therefore, indicates a supernatural action, as if it were a divine intercession. It is necessary to emphasise, again, that the saga of the Ring does not resort only to magical or supernatural elements as a means to win the war. On the contrary, Elves, Dwarves, and Men (including Hobbits) are invited to practice virtue, developing their good qualities, in spite of their limitations, so that Sauron's dominion be overthrown. They are not alone, however. When they find themselves in situations beyond their strength and they show goodwill, they get help as a display of support and consolation.

It is worth mentioning that *The Lord of the Rings* has the

---

74. Tolkien, J.R.R., Carpenter, H. (Org.), Tolkien, C. (Assist.). *The Letters of J.R.R. Tolkien*. Op. cit., Letter 210, p. 271.

elements of a fairy-story and, as such, it has a *eucatastrophic* ending, a happy ending, similar to the gospel narrative that conjoins myth — religiousness filtered through man's imagination — and fact — because it is a historical reality. Thus, the saga of the Ring had its happy outcome, but not without much suffering and the consequences of its brave heroes' weaknesses.

The Ring is destroyed, the Hobbits are welcomed with praise and chanting by all, and Aragorn becomes the King of Gondor. When the Hobbits return to the Shire, they still have to fight off Sharkey (Saruman) and his ruffians, but this conflict also has its eucatastrophic ending, despite the consequences of evil. The happy endings in Tolkienian fairy-stories are not far removed from reality, but also do not indicate a definitive ending, because within Christian faith, which pervades the work even if unconsciously, the true and definitive happy ending can only be found in a metaphysical world, in Heaven.

Eucatastrophe, thus, could not come about without mutual help and collaboration among the free peoples, which favoured the friendly relationships. Each gesture among friends contributed to the happy ending and to the successful outcome of the story, whether definitive or temporary.[75] The destruction of the Ring was possible because all the friends united for the common good and, to do that, they had to somewhat "die" to their own selves in favour of those they loved.

The (not so) happy ending in the lines and on the screen

This separate space will be dedicated to analysing the cinematographic adaptation concerned with the end of the Ring of Power. Peter Jackson's *The Lord of the Rings*: *The Return of the King* was the most internationally awarded entry in the trilogy. Crowning all the movies, it was the one to be awarded eleven Oscar statuettes, something only *Ben Hur* and

---

75. Notice that the stories of Middle-earth are supposed to be, mythologically, our own historical past.

Titanic had achieved before, and four Golden Globe awards: this movie brought about a eucatastrophic ending.

According to the movie producers' documentary in the extended version of the movies, released in 2011 in the USA, the screenwriters Fran Walsh, Philippa Boyens, and the director Peter Jackson had to reorganise the sequence of chapters of *The Two Towers* and *The Return of the King* for the narrative to fit the cinematographic language.

The team noticed that some events that happened in *The Two Towers*, Book III were simultaneous to episodes in *The Return of the King*, Book V. When Frodo is taken by the Orcs and entangled in Shelob's webs (*The Two Towers*, chapter "The Stairs of Cirith Ungol"), at the same time, Gondor is being attacked by Sauron's troops (*The Return of the King*, chapter "The Siege of Gondor") and the steward abandons his post intending to burn himself and his son Faramir.

While Tolkien split the work in "books" (two books for each of the three volumes), telling the story according to the nuclei of the Fellowship, which had been broken, opting to go back and forth in time, the movie producers decided to reorder the facts chronologically, now showing the Men of Rohan and Gondor, then the Hobbits in Mordor. Peter Jackson and his team believed that, by so doing, the spectators would be better off in connecting one fact to the other. Besides, it would be possible to render the scenes more dynamically in cinematic language.

Alexandra Legget, in her thesis *Translating Tolkien: 'The Lord of the Rings' Films as an Imitation, Interpretation, and Emulation of Tolkien's Work*, talks about these three instances of adaptation: imitation, interpretation, and emulation. The first refers to a production concerned with faithfulness, with being the closest possible to the original work; while the latter opens room for a deviation from what is told in the books in favour of a more creative adaptation by the moviemakers. Peter Jackson's movies preserves, to a lesser or greater extent, the three characteristics, even though interpretation seems to dominate:

Thus, in an *interpretation* [from Latin, "interpretation"], the same story is told. However, contrary to an *imitatio* [from Latin, "imitation"], an *interpretatio* does not attempt to utilize the same methods to tell this story. This gives moviemakers the freedom to make points creatively, employing methods conducive to filmmaking and current audiences to explicate well on the story found in the literature.[76]

The moviemakers, then, become the translators of the story, transforming it so that it conforms to the specificities of the seventh art. If that occurs in the organization (whether chronologically or not) of the scenes, it occurs also with the construction, characterization, and representation of the characters. According to Paulo Emílio Salles Gomes, in his essay "A Personagem Cinematográfica" ["The Cinematographic Character"],[77] cinema, like theatre, brings characters that are incarnated in persons, i.e., the actors. For Gomes, it is especially in cinema that we acquire greater intimacy with the protagonists. In a movie, differently from a theatrical spectacle, the actor may become closely associated to the character he or she portrays, particularly when the production becomes a blockbuster. That was the case with *The Lord of the Rings*. Even for those who read Tolkien before Peter Jackson's production, it would be difficult to dissociate Frodo Baggins from the actor Elijah Wood, or even Gandalf from Ian McKellen.

According to Gomes, while the character of a novel is attached to the written words, the movie character depends mostly on its visual representation, even though the words they utter also contribute to it.

One of the most important techniques in cinema is the ellipsis, which is expressed through cutting, framing, and camera movement, among other filmic resources, when the

---

76. Legget, A. *Translating Tolkien: 'The Lord of the Rings' Films as an Imitation, Interpretation, and Emulation of Tolkien's Work.* Master's Thesis. Baylor University, Waco, Texas, 2015, p. 41.
77. Salles, P.E.G. "A Personagem Cinematográfica", in Candido, A. et al. *A Personagem da Ficção.* São Paulo: Perspectiva, 2007.

moviemaker deliberately omits elements aiming to add implicit information to the viewers' conscious/unconscious mind. The ellipsis technique helps the spectator capture what is being shown by completing elements that are intentionally absent in the filmic production. "Capable of showing everything and knowing the formidable tenor of reality that impregnates everything appearing on the screen, the moviemaker can resort to allusions and making themself understood evasively".[78]

Marcel Martin, in his book *A Linguagem Cinematográfica* [Cinematographic Language, from the original *Le Language Cinématografique*] reminds that, wherever one finds artistic activity, there will also be a choice, and that the moviemaker, the playwright, and the writer make their choices and put them in a certain order. As Tolkien had done, Peter Jackson chose the order of the events in his work to tell the same story, having in mind the message he wanted to convey through that medium (movie screens, videos). To do that, the producers resorted to decoupage, which consists of "choosing the fragments of reality that are going to be created by the camera".[79] After that, each fragment is synthetically attached in the montage.

Another cinema technique related to ellipsis which will be considered a little further is that of linking and transitions: "In a movie, the objective of transitions is to ensure narrative fluidity and to avoid erroneous concatenations (axis break)".[80]

We are now going to take a closer look at the movie, establishing a relationship between the chapter "Mount Doom", in *The Return of the King*, and its correspondent scene in the movie. We will observe the sequence showing the outcome of the Quest, the eucatastrophic ending against the Ring and its creator, Sauron, emphasising the importance of friendship (personal and political) for his defeat. To do so, we will also draw from chapters whose events happen simultaneously, or immediately before and after, such as "The Last Debate", "The

---

78. Martin, M. *A Linguagem Cinematográfica*. São Paulo: Brasiliense, 2011, p. 83.
79. Id., p. 85.
80. Id., p. 97.

Black Gate Opens", and "The Field of Cormallen", taking into consideration the cuts between scenes as proposed by the movie version.

Intercut battles

The movie adaptation evidently deviates in some respects from the literary text. The actions in the chapter "Mount Doom" are split in two episodes of the movie: "The Tower of Cirith Ungol" and "The End of All Things", an interval of about thirty minutes, which includes information from preceding chapters of the book (including from the second volume, *The Two Towers*) or succeeding ones.

In the movie, Sam and Frodo's journey is interposed by battle scenes with the Captains of the West, led by Aragorn, against Sauron's troops, in front of the Black Gates, as a means to attract the Dark Lord's attention. In the book, the same scenes are divided in parts (which the author calls "Books", six in all), and the reader has to go back in the narrative timeline and the pages to establish a connection between the events.

The last volume of the saga, *The Return of the King*, for instance, is divided in Books V and VI. Book V tells the adventures of the members of the Fellowship of the Ring that have been left behind by the Ring-bearer — Aragorn, Gimli, Gandalf, Legolas, Merry, and Pippin — and it mostly relates the episodes concerned with the battles and their consequences. Book VI tells the story of the Ring's destruction with Frodo, Sam, and Gollum, and the outcome of the saga. This allows the reader to go deep into what Frodo and Sam experienced *and* what the other heroes, distant from the Ring, experienced. Thus, no part is overshadowed by the other; on the contrary, there is an exchange between them, and each separated group of the Fellowship adds to the other — the deeds of the two Hobbits are emphasised, though, since the Ring, the great driving force of the plot, is with them.

In the movie, the scenes are synchronically presented,

with intercuts. Such a resource emphasises, from the point of view of movie language, the hypothesis that the action among friends favoured the successful outcome, as well as suggests that heroism in Tolkien's story is multiple — and, at the same time, often faltering. The book, in this sense, is more analytical and contemplative, while the movie is more synthetic and dynamic, provoking in the viewer more sensations than pauses for reflection.

In the chapter "The Last Debate" (*The Return of the King*), Gandalf, Aragorn, the prince Imrahil of Dol Amroth, Éomer, and the sons of Elrond — Elrohir and Elladan — the so-called Captains of the West, discuss, after the Battle of the Fields of Pelennor, what should be done to stop Sauron and gain time to let Frodo and Sam fulfil the Quest. At that moment, Gandalf exposes his plan against Sauron: the wizard proposes to attract the enemy's attention and, thus, he will not notice the Hobbits' presence.

Let us see the passage of the book and, afterwards, the dialogue transcribed from the movie, so that we can make a critical analysis of both languages. Gandalf says:

> […] Without [the Ring] we cannot by force defeat his force. But we must at all costs keep his Eye from his true peril. *We cannot achieve victory by arms, but by arms we can give the Ring-bearer his only chance*, frail though it be.[81]

Before proceeding, we will examine some concepts in the Istar's speech. As we have seen, the greatest weapon brought by the wizard to Middle-earth was the instruction and concepts connected to wisdom, important in making decisions of ethical nature. That is why he says "We cannot achieve victory by arms".

The greatest triumph over the Enemy lies in values that do not depend on armed strife: it lies, most of all, on mercy. However, the need for physical struggle is real, and Gandalf

---

81. Tolkien, J.R.R. *The Lord of the Rings*. Op. cit., p. 1151, emphasis added.

adds: "but by arms we can give the Ring-bearer his only chance". Such a concept can be summed up in the saying uttered by the captain of Gondor, Faramir, to Frodo, when the Hobbits and Gollum enter his domain without permission, in the chapter "The Window on the West":

> War must be, while we defend our lives against a destroyer who would devour all; but I do not love the bright sword for its sharpness, nor the arrow for its swiftness, nor the warrior for his glory. I love only that which they defend [...].[82]

Back to the dialogue between Gandalf and the Captains of the West, before they set off to challenge Sauron in front of the Front Gates, he adds:

> '*As Aragorn has begun, so we must go on.* We must push Sauron to his last throw. [...]' 'We must walk open-eyed into that trap, with courage, but small hope for ourselves. [...] But this, I deem, is our duty. And better so than to perish nonetheless – as we surely shall, if we sit here – and know as we die that no new age shall be.'[83]

As pointed out by the wizard, there was little hope in the success of the tactic deployed by the members of the broken Fellowship. However, this was their role in the story, and the friendship among peoples was proven, fulfilling their mission, giving their lives to their friends.

Comparing the dialogue in the movie and the corresponding passage of the book, we notice some differences not only because of the shift in medium, but also due to some changes in the portrayal of the characters. The biggest change happens with the wizard Gandalf. The movie team chose to portray him slightly more hesitant in this scene, while Aragorn is more confident and braver.

As we saw, it is Gandalf, with his usual wisdom and self-confidence, who suggests, in the book, that they go to Sauron's

---

82. Tolkien, J.R.R. *The Lord of the Rings*. Op. cit., p. 878.
83. Id, pp. 1151-1152.

gates to attract his attention. When the wizard speaks, in the book, about the threat of defeat if they all go to the Black Gates to fight the Enemy, it does not mean, for instance, that he is afraid, as the movie conveys: his speech reinforces the great peril that comes with that decision and, therefore, the great courage of the combatants in making it happen.

In the movie, however, it is Aragorn who proposes that. The explanation for this choice is twofold: first because Aragorn had already used this strategy of attracting Sauron's attention outside Mordor. *In the book*, in this very same chapter "The Last Debate", a little before Gandalf's suggestion, the wizard talks to the future king in front of his friends:

> 'Now Sauron knows all this, and he knows that this precious thing which he lost has been found again; but he does not yet know where it is, or so we hope. [...] Aragorn, that you have shown yourself to him in the Stone of Orthanc?'
> 'I did so ere I rode from the Hornburg,' answered Aragorn. 'I deemed that the time was ripe, and that the Stone had come to me for just such a purpose. It was then ten days since the Ring-bearer went east from Rauros, and *the Eye of Sauron, I thought, should be drawn out from his own land.* Too seldom has he been challenged since he returned to his Tower.'[84]

The Stone of Orthanc, a palantír, was a seeing stone that, among other things, enabled one to attract Sauron's Eye when one held it. Aragorn showed himself to it so that the Enemy learned his whereabouts — since he was hated for being Isildur's heir, who cut the Ring off Sauron's hand and defeated him in the battle of the Gladden Fields — and, thus, deviate his attention from Frodo Baggins to the future king.

The second reason for giving Aragorn prominence in the scene was the intention to put the future king of Gondor as the main agent in the plan to fight before the Black Gates north of Mordor's entrance. Thus, Aragorn's figure would be stronger and more impactful in the movie.

---

84. Id., pp. 1150-1151, emphasis added.

Peter Jackson's team even filmed a scene in which Sauron assumed the shape of Annatar, an alias of Sauron in the Second Age, when he assumed a fair appearance to win the trust of the Elves in Eregion and convince them to forge the rings, without revealing his true intentions. This is how he is described in *The Silmarillion*:

[Sauron] found the easiest to sway of all the peoples of the Earth; but long he sought to persuade the Elves to his service, for he knew that the Firstborn had the greater power [...]

[...] for Sauron took to himself *the name of Annatar, the Lord of Gifts*, and they had at first much profit from his friendship. [...]

Now the Elves made many rings; but secretly Sauron made One Ring to rule all the others [...][85]

The intention of the movie team was to intercalate the scene in which Aragorn fought Annatar — who would afterwards reveal himself as Sauron — with that of Frodo and Sam, who were taking the Ring to the Cracks of Doom. However, the team realised that, if they did that, the Hobbits' actions would be obfuscated, giving the impression that Aragorn was the hero of the story and the main agent in Sauron's final defeat.

Tolkien was clear in his letters that *The Lord of the Rings* "had been planned to be 'hobbito-centric', that is, primarily a study of the ennoblement (or sanctification) of the humble".[86] Responsive to that, the moviemakers decided to show Aragorn's strength in another way: fighting a Mountain-troll.

It is worth remembering, however, that it is the Hobbit Pippin who, in the book, kills a troll in a fight. Thus, his greatness was equalised with Merry's, who helped Éowyn, the maiden of Rohan, to kill the Witch-King of Angmar, the leader of the Nazgûl — because of that, he did not take part in the Battle of the Morannon, since he stayed in the Houses of Healing.

In the movie, after the discussion among Gandalf, Legolas,

---

85. Tolkien, J.R.R. *The Silmarillion*. Op. cit., pp.343-344.
86. Tolkien, J.R.R., Carpenter, H. (Org.), Tolkien, C. (Assist.). *The Letters of J.R.R. Tolkien*. Op. cit., Letter 181, p. 237.

Gimli, Aragorn, and Éomer, and the cut showing them setting off to the battle, the viewer is shown the troops of Orcs heading to the Black Gates. Frodo and Sam, in the movie, see the enemies from a distance, while, in the book, they follow the Orcs in disguise until they manage to escape. That is how the scene is described in the chapter "The Land of Shadow":

> Along all the roads troops were moving; for the Captains of the West were advancing and the Dark Lord was speeding his forces north. [...] A troop of heavy-armed uruks from Barad-dûr charged into the Durthang line and threw them into confusion.
> Dazed as he was with pain and weariness, Sam woke up, grasped quickly at his chance, and threw himself to the ground, dragging Frodo down with him. Orcs fell over them, snarling and cursing. Slowly on hand and knee the hobbits crawled away out of the turmoil, until at last unnoticed they dropped over the further edge of the road.[87]

If the Uruks from Barad-dûr had not charged against the Durthang Orcs, the Hobbits would not have been able to crawl away from the troops. Once again, we see that in Tolkien's works evil makes everything more difficult for itself, because the enemies of the free peoples often fight among themselves and are characterised by strife and treason. Such attitudes help the reader understand better who the Enemy and his servants are, because there is constant strife between them, and that is precisely Sauron's greatest desire: that the free peoples destroy themselves through internal disruption, becoming, thus, enemies.

In the movie *The Return of the King*, the issue of strife among enemies is portrayed in other scenes, such as in the one where Frodo is held captive in the tower of Cirith Ungol and the Orcs fight for his belongings, similarly to what is described in *The Two Towers* book. The scene in which Frodo and Sam escape from the Orcs because of their internal strife is not shown in the movie. It may have been that the moviemakers thought it would

---

87. Tolkien, J.R.R. *The Lord of the Rings*. Op. cit., p. 1219.

be redundant, in terms of cinematographic language, to repeat very similar episodes. Besides, the cinematographic structure privileges the condensation of ideas and, as such, it often resorts to artifices such as ellipsis and metaphor. One cannot disregard, however, that the absence of these scenes in the movie can be damaging to the sense and essence of the story.

The sequence of events, then, starts to show the Hobbits' struggle to reach the heart of Mordor. From the last chapter of the second volume, "The Choices of Master Samwise", on, the episodes involving Frodo and Sam, even though narrated by a third-person narrator, show their adventures according to Sam's view.

According to Nikolajeva,[88] this type of character is the focaliser: while the text is written in the third person, it goes into the mind of a character. From the moment Sam finds himself alone, until the destruction of the Ring, we follow his thoughts closely. He assumes the role of hero and shows his worldview to the readers. Such a change in focus suggests that Samwise Gamgee himself wrote or edited these passages in the Red Book, a plausible hypothesis since Frodo was unconscious in the Tower of Cirith Ungol, and completely disturbed in Mordor, which would supposedly affect his memories about the events.

This is not so evident in the movie adaptation. Frodo's suffering in Mount Doom is more fully explored, and Sam remains his faithful friend, like a batman in his supporting role. Gamgee still has an important part in the movie, but the protagonism is split, and most of the attention lies on Frodo. One could hypothesise that this choice was made so that the audience would not find it strange that the story does not have a single hero or that the protagonism is transferred, something very uncommon in Hollywoodian narratives. It is worth reminding that most Awards nominate a single actor per production in the category of best protagonist, and this role has always been seen as Elijah Wood's in *The Lord of the Rings*.

---

88. Nikolajeva, M. *The Rhetoric of Character in Children's Literature*. Op. cit.

In the book, however, we insist on the fact that the events are related more and more according to Sam's view, who becomes the protagonist of the story. Already in the beginning of the chapter "Mount Doom", we follow his thoughts:

> Sam put his ragged orc-cloak under his master's head, and covered them both with the grey robe of Lórien; and as he did so his thoughts went out to that fair land, and to the Elves, and he hoped that the cloth woven by their hands might have some virtue to keep them hidden beyond all hope in this wilderness of fear. [...]
> Sam took a sip of water, but pressed Frodo to drink, and when his master had recovered a little he gave him a whole wafer of their precious waybread and made him eat it.[89]

Full of compassion for his friend, Sam displays his mercy by attending to Frodo's physical needs, as preached by the Christians: feed the hungry, give drink to the thirsty, clothe the naked, shelter the pilgrims, come to the ill and the prisoners, and bury the dead.[90]

We see a correspondent scene in the movie when Frodo tries to drink water but finds his bottle empty. Sam offers his own bottle:

> Sam: *Take mine... there's a few drops left.*
> Frodo: *There'll be none left for the return journey.*
> Sam: *I don't think there will be a return journey, Mr. Frodo.*

Gamgee's claim that he does not believe there will be a return journey refers to what Sam says in the book:

> Never for long had hope died in his staunch heart, and always until now he had taken some thought for their return. But the bitter truth came home to him at last: at best their provision would take them

89. Tolkien, J.R.R. *The Lord of the Rings*. Op. cit., p. 1220.
90. Cf. Matthew 25: 34-37: "Then shall the King say unto them on his right hand, Come, ye blessed of my Father, inherit the kingdom prepared for you from the foundation of the world: For I was an hungred, and ye gave me meat: I was thirsty, and ye gave me drink: I was a stranger, and ye took me in: Naked, and ye clothed me: I was sick, and ye visited me: I was in prison, and ye came unto me."

to their goal; and when the task was done, there they would come to an end, alone, houseless, foodless in the midst of a terrible desert. There could be no return.[91]

But these thoughts are not permanent: many times, Sam oscillates between hope and despondency, now experiencing comfort, and then fear and bitterness. This fluctuation of ideas demonstrates the growth of the character, who, along with the reader, suffers the consequences of Sauron's hostile lands, but, at the same time, grows in bravery and steadiness, regardless of the ordeals he goes through.

'So that was the job I felt I had to do when I started,' thought Sam: 'to help Mr. Frodo to the last step and then die with him? Well, if that is the job then I must do it. [...] I can't think somehow that Gandalf would have sent Mr. Frodo on this errand, if there hadn't a' been any hope of his ever coming back at all. [...]
But even as hope died in Sam, or seemed to die, it was turned to a new strength. [...]
With a new sense of responsibility he brought his eyes back to the ground near at hand, studying the next move.[92]

The chapter "Mount Doom" was adapted by Peter Jackson and his team basically by intercalating passages of it with those of the chapter "The Black Gate Opens", when the Battle of the Morannon takes place. The scenes of battle, which alternate with that of Frodo and Sam in Mount Doom, reinforce the Hobbits' mission, carrying the Ring with them, the greatest burden of the war against the Enemy.

In the movie, after Sam gives water to Frodo and stretches out his hand so that he can stand up, there is a cut to the army of the free peoples, standing watchful, ready for battle. Afterwards, we go back to Frodo, who holds the Ring with his right hand and gestures quickly with his left one, so that we associate Frodo's tension before the peril, and the storm that his friends were facing in front of the Black Gates:

91. Tolkien, J.R.R. *The Lord of the Rings*. Op. cit., p. 1221.
92. Id., p. 1221, emphasis added.

Anxiously *Sam had noted how his master's left hand would often be raised* as if to ward off a blow, or to screen his shrinking eyes from a dreadful Eye that sought to look in them. *And sometimes his right hand would creep to his breast*, clutching, and then slowly, as the will recovered mastery, it would be withdrawn.[93]

Just as it happens in the book, the scene goes on showing the action of Sauron's Eye moving along with Frodo. Peter Jackson chose to represent Sauron, most of the time, without a concrete physical form, only as an eye. In the beginning of the first movie, *The Fellowship of the Ring*, he appears with a humanoid body, fighting Isildur. Afterwards, he is only portrayed as a fiery eye on top of his tower.

It is not true, however, that Sauron lost his physical form after Isildur took the Ring from his finger, and the references to him as an Eye are metaphorical rather than concrete. This is what we learn in the chapter "The Shadow of the Past": "Then Sauron was vanquished and his spirit fled and was hidden for long years, until his shadow took shape again in Mirkwood".[94]

In a letter, Tolkien makes it even clearer that Sauron has a physical form: "Sauron should be thought of as very terrible. The form that he took was that of a man of more than human stature, but not gigantic".[95] Elsewhere, in another letter, the author also explains the mythology around Sauron and his relationship with the physical body, considering that he had fought other battles during the Second Age:

It is mythologically supposed that when this shape was 'real', [...], it took some time to build up. It was then destructible like other physical organisms. But that of course did not destroy the spirit, nor dismiss it from the world to which it was bound until the end. After the battle with Gil-galad and Elendil, Sauron took a long while to re-build, longer than he had done after the Downfall of Númenor (I suppose because each building-up used up some of the inherent

93. Id., pp. 1223-1224, emphasis added.
94. Id., pp. 68-69.
95. Tolkien, J.R.R., Carpenter, H. (Org.), Tolkien, C. (Assist.). *The Letters of J.R.R. Tolkien.* Op. cit., Letter 246, p. 332.

energy of the spirit, which might be called the 'will' or the effective link between the indestructible mind and being and the realization of its imagination). The impossibility of re-building after the destruction of the Ring, is sufficiently clear 'mythologically' in the present book.[96]

It is pertinent to remember that the literary version — and its correspondent movie passage — in which Frodo protects the Ring with his right hand, pushes away the malignant forces with his left one, and falls over by the action of the Eye, is connected to a further passage, in the chapter "Mount Doom":

The Eye was not turned to them: it was gazing north to where the Captains of the West stood at bay, and thither all its malice was now bent, as the Power moved to strike its deadly blow; *but Frodo at that dreadful glimpse fell as one stricken mortally.* His hand sought the chain about his neck.[97]

In the movie, after Frodo collapses to the ground feeling Sauron's Eye, what we witness is precisely the scene with the army of the Captains of the West. In the foreground we see Pippin's face, then Aragorn, Gandalf, and Legolas; after that, a cut to a long shot, showing the knights approaching the Gates, trying to attract Sauron's attention to themselves, deviating it from Frodo and the Ring.

The tension remains, because Frodo is still lying on the ground, hoping not to be seen by the Eye. After that, the Captains are shown through a high-angle shot, giving the impression that Sauron looks at them from above.

Up until then, the interplay of images is enough to show what the story conveys, and the information contained in dialogues is, *a priori*, eschewed. But, suddenly, Aragorn speaks before the gates, since in the movie it seems that Aragorn, and not Gandalf, is in charge:

---

96. Tolkien, J.R.R., Carpenter, H. (Org.), Tolkien, C. (Assist.). *The Letters of J.R.R. Tolkien.* Op. cit., Letter 200, p. 260.
97. Tolkien, J.R.R. *The Lord of the Rings.* Op. cit., p. 1233, emphasis added.

Aragorn: *Let the lord of the Black Land come forth! Let justice be done upon him!*

In the book, the chapter "The Black Gate Opens" has the following:

> When all was ordered, the Captains rode forth towards the Black Gate with a great guard of horsemen and the banner and heralds and trumpeters. There was Gandalf as chief herald, and Aragorn with the sons of Elrond, and Éomer of Rohan, and Imrahil; and Legolas and Gimli and Peregrin were bidden to go also, so that all the enemies of Mordor should have a witness. [...]
> 'Come forth!' they cried. 'Let the Lord of the Black Land come forth! Justice shall be done upon him.'[98]

Despite Aragorn's great leadership in battle, the attention is, in the book, split among the characters, and Gandalf is described as the "chief herald". The moviemakers chose to focus on the future king because they understood that the character's strength would be more evident — and because of the greater commercial appeal, in a classical hero/heartthrob scene, interpreted by Viggo Mortensen, who goes through war to conquer the love of a woman — the fair Elf Arwen, played by Liv Tyler.

After the opening of the Gates, the Eye moves towards them, in a low-angle shot, giving the impression that the warriors are small in comparison to him, and how close he seems to be. After that, it is shown that Sauron turned his look away from the Hobbits within his land. The plan of the Captains of the West seems to have had a successful beginning.

Another scene concerning the battle in front of the Gates follows, in which Sauron's messengers approach, keeping Aragorn's army at bay, the two Hobbits get up. Sam tells Frodo that the light of Sauron's Eye is now to the North.

There is another cut to the battle, and Aragorn's speech follows:

---

98. Id., p. 1162.

Aragorn: *Sons of Gondor – of Rohan... my brothers.*
I see in your eyes the same fear that would take the heart of me.
The day may come when the courage of Men fails...
When we forsake our friends and break all bonds of fellowship.
But it is not this day.
An hour of wolves and shattered shields...
When the Age of Man comes crashing down.
But it is not this day!
This day we fight!
By all that you hold dear on this good earth...
I bid you stand, Men of the West!

Aragorn's speech reinforces our hypothesis that friendship is a crucial factor for the victory against Sauron: "*The day may come when the courage of Men fails... When we forsake our friends and break all bonds of fellowship. But it is not this day.*" Arathorn's son bid his friends unite because it is by friendship that their peoples will have some chance, even if slim, of surviving. The future king's speech also indicates the connection between friendship and a happy ending (eucatastrophe), showing how the absence of this kind of love can bring about a tragic end: "*An hour of wolves and shattered shields... When the Age of Man comes crashing down*".

Meanwhile, Frodo and Sam have gotten up and resumed their walking. But their suffering is great, and they constantly stumble or fall over. The torment experienced by both Hobbits, especially Frodo, due to his burden, is emphasised in the movie adaptation. This can also be seen in the setting, which portrays the deserted, sombre environment of Mordor.

The dark and reddish lighting also contributes to the austerity of the scene, not to mention the art direction resources such as costume design and make-up, rendering their clothes shabby and their bodies filthy. The close-ups intensify the drama of the action, highlighting the actors' work and imparting the same tension and suffering of the characters to the spectator. The cuts between scenes prevail, as if Frodo and Sam's struggle were symbolised by the battle of Men who approach the enemy troops.

Anticipating what might befall, Legolas and Gimli have a short dialogue that reinforces the bonds of friendship both from the collective point of view of their peoples, and the intimate, personal one:

Gimli: *Never thought I'd die fighting side by side with an Elf.*
Legolas: *What about side by side with a friend?*
Gimli: *Aye – I could do that.*

The following scene shows Sam crawling on the mountain after his fallen friend: the dialogue of friendship between Legolas and Gimli is, then, connected to the gestures between the Hobbits in Mordor. Even though the movie does not show Sam's thoughts, as it occurs in the book, his presence is also memorable because it is evident that, without him, Frodo would have succumbed even before entering the Cracks of Doom.

Despite the morbid environment in Mordor, Sam tries to bring hope to his friend, reminding him of the Shire to encourage him, rescuing the memory of home and of what they considered happy and peaceful:

Sam: *Do you remember the Shire, Mr. Frodo? It'll be spring soon, and the orchards will be in blossom; and the birds will be nesting in the hazel thicket; and they'll be sowing the summer barley in the lower fields; and eating the first of the strawberries with cream. Do you remember the taste of strawberries?*
Frodo: *No, Sam. I can't recall the taste of food; nor the sound of water; nor the touch of grass. I'm naked in the dark. There's no veil between me and the wheel of fire. I can see it with my waking eyes.*

The movie dialogue was probably inspired in the following conversation between the Hobbits in the book:

'Do you remember that bit of rabbit, Mr. Frodo?' he said. 'And our place under the warm bank in Captain Faramir's country, the day I saw an oliphaunt?'

'No, I am afraid not, Sam,' said Frodo. 'At least, I know that such things happened, but I cannot see them. No taste of food, no feel of water, no sound of wind, no memory of tree or grass or flower, no image of moon or star are left to me. I am naked in the dark, Sam, and there is no veil between me and the wheel of fire. I begin to see it even with my waking eyes, and all else fades.'[99]

This and other moments during their struggle to reach Mount Doom show how Sam brings, or tries to bring, an enlivening force into Frodo. Even in a gloomy and desperate situation, the gardener is the one who tries to make his master and friend smile, and he succeeds, sometimes, despite frequent frustration. This is also a typical feature of friendship, which tries to reach a truce of hope amid tragedy.

In the movie adaptation, Sam soon tries to cheer him up, as opposed to what happens in the book, where Gamgee will still go through many doubts and attempts to regain determination, apart from many internal dialogues and external signs of hope.

> Sam: *Then let us be rid of it – once and for all! Come on, Mr. Frodo. I can't carry it for you... but I can carry you! Come on!*

The scene is climactic and the actors' interpretation — Elijah Wood as Frodo and Sean Astin as Sam — impart emotion to it, along with the crescendo of the soundtrack, which gives the impression that the characters — and spectators — are reanimating and regaining hope, despite all the suffering. The corresponding passage in the book is very similar to it:

> 'Come, Mr. Frodo!' he cried. 'I can't carry it for you, but I can carry you and it as well. So up you get! Come on, Mr. Frodo dear! Sam will give you a ride. Just tell him where to go, and he'll go.'[100]

The consequence of Sam's action to Frodo was surprising: instead of becoming even wearier, Gamgee seemed to acquire supernatural help because of his action of mercy:

---

99. Tolkien, J.R.R. *The Lord of the Rings*. Op. cit., p. 1226.
100. Id., p. 1230.

Whether because Frodo was so worn by his long pains, wound
of knife, and venomous sting, and sorrow, fear, and homeless
wandering, or because some gift of final strength was given to him,
Sam lifted Frodo with no more difficulty than if he were carrying
a hobbit-child pig-a-back in some romp on the lawns or hayfields
of the Shire.[101]

The above quotation highlights two issues: Frodo's worn
physical and mental state and a potential supernatural or magical
help that favours their mission. In this sense, Tolkien gives the
readers freedom to interpret. They may or may not believe that
supernatural forces interfered. He does hint, however, at his
literary Subcreation when we search for further answers: the
superior spiritual forces do exist in Arda and, somehow, they
exert their influence in Middle-earth, as evidenced by the very
presence of Gandalf himself.

The episode can lead us to an interpretation based on
Christian concepts, as the gospel passage suggests: "Take my
yoke upon you, and learn of me; for I am meek and lowly in
heart: and ye shall find rest unto your souls. For my yoke is
easy, and my burden is light." When Sam decides to take up
the burden of carrying his friend, to his surprise everything
becomes light — even if for a brief moment — as if the result
of his attitude symbolised the lightness of his conscience, his
state of spirit.

After this touching scene in the adaptation, there is a cut to
a long shot of Mount Doom and, at a distant point, attentive
viewers can spot Gollum exploring among the rocks. The
following scene goes back to the battle. Aragorn notices a
flash of light on top of the tower. Sauron calls him, first by the
name Aragorn, and then Elessar (the Elfstone), the name that
would be given to him after being confirmed King. According
to the moviemaking team, this scene would initially precede
the encounter between Aragorn and Annatar, later revealed
as Sauron. This scene, as mentioned, was aborted, but the

101.Id., pp. 1230-1231.

beginning was included. The outcome, however, was different: the future king turns to his friends, saying "For Frodo" and heads to the strife.

The change in the scene is drastic but remains somewhat close to the literary character. It is the two Hobbits that deserve attention and, at least in the sequence from the destruction of the Ring to the rescue by the Eagles, Frodo is praised by all the free peoples.

After Aragorn hurtles towards Sauron's troops, all the soldiers of the free peoples also move towards the battle. The music grows and the images are also dynamic.

Cut to the scene of the two Hobbits, with Sam still carrying Frodo on his back, when they are waylaid by Gollum, who says *"Clever Hobbits to climb so high!"*. After that, Gollum struggles with Frodo, trying to snatch the Ring exactly when he was almost entering the crack of the mountain. Filled with anger, the vile creature tries to strangle Frodo. He is too exhausted to fight, and it is Sam who saves him, throwing a rock at Gollum. In the book, the outlook is different:

> [...] Sam saw these two rivals with other vision. A crouching shape, scarcely more than the shadow of a living thing, a creature now wholly ruined and defeated, yet filled with a hideous lust and rage; and before it stood stern, untouchable now by pity, a figure robed in white, but at its breast it held a wheel of fire. Out of the fire there spoke a commanding voice.
>
> 'Begone, and trouble me no more! If you touch me ever again, you shall be cast yourself into the Fire of Doom.'[102]

Tolkien sought to show how the power of the Ring transformed Frodo: "stood stern, untouchable now by pity, a figure robed in white, but at its breast it held a wheel of fire". Peter Jackson, on the other hand, tried to show Baggins's exhaustion when he is attacked. The portrayal of Gollum, however, is similar to that of the book: a "crouching shape, scarcely more than the shadow of a living thing, a creature

102. Tolkien, J.R.R. *The Lord of the Rings.* Op. cit., pp. 1234-1235.

now wholly ruined and defeated, yet filled with a hideous lust and rage".

A crucial difference between the literary text and the movie is Sam's reaction before Gollum. After Frodo escapes his opponent, Sam has the chance of killing his opponent, but that he does not do:

> Sam's hand wavered. His mind was hot with wrath and the memory of evil. It would be just to slay this treacherous, murderous creature, just and many times deserved; and also it seemed the only safe thing to do. *But deep in his heart there was something that restrained him*: he could not strike this thing lying in the dust, forlorn, ruinous, utterly wretched. *He himself, though only for a little while, had borne the Ring, and now dimly he guessed the agony of Gollum's shrivelled mind and body, enslaved to that Ring, unable to find peace or relief ever in life again.* But Sam had no words to express what he felt.[103]

The fact that Sam was, briefly, a Ring-bearer, enables him to notice the hard time Gollum was going through: by recognising his misery, having borne the Bane of Isildur for some moments, Sam learned to forgive, the most sublime attitude of mercy. However, this attitude towards Gollum was too late:[104] at that moment, the vile creature would regret nothing.

The sequence of the movie shows increasingly more intense and related scenes, thus reinforcing the importance of friendship to the fulfilling of the Quest. While the Hobbits fight with Gollum, takes of the battle are shown: blows, stabs, and other war movements appear on the screen. Amid the turmoil, Gandalf sees the Nazgûl approaching in their winged beasts (called nazgûl-birds or "fell beasts"). At the same time, he sees a moth, a sign of hope that refers to a connection with the supernatural. On the other side, an eagle appears and starts to fight with a nazgûl-bird, symbolising the struggle between Good and Evil.

---

103. Id., p. 1235, emphasis added.
104. Tolkien wrote in a letter: "this seems to me really like the real world in which the instruments of just retribution are seldom themselves just or holy; and the good are often stumbling blocks." (*The Letters of J.R.R. Tolkien.* Op. cit., Letter 165, p. 221)

Attracting the Nazgûl is important because they were the only ones who could warn Sauron about the danger. The battle was, therefore, essential to attract all the forces of evil, whether intelligent or not. The eagles are a sign of good omens, meaning hope, divine help, the triumph over Evil. Their presence gives energy and hope to those in battle. In the book, they appear only at the end of the battle, when Pippin defeats the troll and, just like in the movie — and despite the fact that he did not defeat the troll, as in the book — the Hobbit cries: "'The Eagles are coming! The Eagles are coming!'".[105]

The Climax of the (non) hero

The movie scene of Frodo and Sam at the crack of Sammath Naur, in Mount Doom, is similar to the book episode: Sam finds Frodo by the edge of the abyss, and the tension grows because all he has to do is to throw the Ring in the fire, and nothing, apparently, prevents him from doing so. This is what the book tells:

> [...] at the very Crack of Doom, stood Frodo, black against the glare, tense, erect, but still as if he had been turned to stone.
> 'Master!' cried Sam.
> Then Frodo stirred and spoke with a clear voice, indeed with a voice clearer and more powerful than Sam had ever heard him use [...].
> 'I have come,' he said. 'But I do not choose now to do what I came to do. I will not do this deed. The Ring is mine!' And suddenly, as he set it on his finger, he vanished from Sam's sight.[106]

Similarly, the movie plays with close-ups to build tension, and Frodo and Sam have a dialogue:

Sam: *Frodo!*
Frod: *I'm here, Sam.*
Sam: *Destroy it – go on! Throw it in the fire! What are you waiting*

105. Tolkien, J.R.R. *The Lord of the Rings*. Op. cit., p. 1169.
106. Id., p. 1237.

for? Just let it go!
Frodo: *The Ring is mine.*
[Frodo pulls the Ring from the chain and puts it on]
Sam: *No. No.*
[Frodo disappears]
Sam: *No!*
[At this moment, the Eye turns from the battle to the Mountain.
Immediately, the Nazgûl abandon the battle and head to Orodruin]

The corresponding passage in the book is explored more in
regard to the Enemy's reaction:

> The Dark Lord was suddenly aware of him, and his Eye piercing all
> shadows looked across the plain to the door that he had made; and
> the magnitude of his own folly was revealed to him in a blinding
> flash, and all the devices of his enemies were at last laid bare. Then
> his wrath blazed in consuming flame, but his fear rose like a vast
> black smoke to choke him. [...]
>   At his summons, wheeling with a rending cry, in a last desperate
> race there flew, faster than the winds, the Nazgûl, the Ringwraiths,
> and with a storm of wings they hurtled southwards to Mount
> Doom.[107]

The book describes Sauron's fear at that moment, because
he knew the great risk he was running by finding out that the
Captains of the West did not have his Ring, and that if the
magical object was destroyed, so was he. In the heart of the
Mountain, Frodo was powerful enough to lead the Dark Lord
and his Nazgûl into despair.

After that episode, in the movie, Frodo's footprints on the
mountain appear, because he is now invisible with the Ring.
Just like in the book, Gollum strikes Sam's head and follows
Frodo's footprints, and another struggle for the Ring ensues,
right on the edge of the abyss. The strife between Frodo and
Gollum becomes more thrilling with intercuts of the battle, in
which Aragorn fights the Mountain-troll.

The production team allowed many attempts to demonstrate

---

107. Id., pp. 1237-1238.

the struggle between Frodo and Gollum. The first time, they rendered it more violently, giving the impression that Baggins pushed Gollum on purpose, killing him voluntarily. Afterwards, they realised that this would impart extreme aggressiveness to Frodo, and that it was not his nature to pour hatred upon Gollum. Indeed, this would give a misleading impression of the character because, as we saw, his heroism did not depend on destroying the Ring or not, but on being compassionate and merciful towards Gollum.

At last, the scene acquired a new configuration, more coherent with Frodo Baggins, even though significant changes from the book are observed. After Gollum bit his finger, Frodo reappears and screams, collapsing to the ground, horrified. Gollum becomes ecstatic, obsessed with the Ring, and this process takes some time — supposedly due to the slow motion, while, in the background, we hear a melodious tune — until Frodo gets to his feet and struggles once again with Gollum, and both slip into the abyss.

The tense atmosphere increases because the spectator does not know what happened to them. Gollum appears, then, in slow motion, falling into the abyss and absorbed in his precious. Finally, he dives into the lava but, contrary to what one would expect, the Ring is not destroyed.

Peter Jackson and his team, then, opted to leave the destruction of the Ring completely in Frodo's hands. He had not fallen into the abyss, but was hanging. At that moment, the fate of all Middle-earth is not upon Frodo's decisions alone, but also in the value he gives to Sam's friendship.

Hanging by a thread, Frodo sees his friend reaching out his hand to him. The atmosphere grows in tension once again, and Sam insists on reaching out his hand. The camera closes on the characters' faces and hands, and cuts to close-ups on the Ring too, which floats on the lava and now shines brighter, revealing its inscriptions. This image interplay reinforces the idea that the destruction lies with Frodo, who must decide between friendship and his attachment to his own self, since the Ring symbolises the Universal Self.

Finally, the Hobbit chooses to give his hand to his friend, and the Ring is destroyed. Similar to what happens in the book, Sauron's Eye is annihilated, and everything in Mordor collapses.

In the book, however, the sequence of actions is faster and less tense, even a little frustrating for those who followed the suffering of the Hobbits until they reached the Cracks of Doom:

> Suddenly Sam saw Gollum's long hands draw upwards to his mouth; his white fangs gleamed, and then snapped as they bit. Frodo gave a cry, and there he was, fallen upon his knees at the chasm's edge. But Gollum, dancing like a mad thing, held aloft the ring, a finger still thrust within its circle. It shone now as if verily it was wrought of living fire.
>
> 'Precious, precious, precious!' Gollum cried. 'My Precious! O my Precious!' And with that, even as his eyes were lifted up to gloat on his prize, he stepped too far, toppled, wavered for a moment on the brink, and then with a shriek he fell. Out of the depths came his last wail *Precious*, and he was gone.[108]

It is clear that the importance of friendship, in the book, is seen mostly on the long way they travelled, which is consolidated at the end: Samwise Gamgee is, to the last minute, besides Frodo; and to this very moment the Captains of the West and the army of the free peoples are battling against the Enemy in front of the Black Gates. In the movie, however, the importance of the friendship must be reinforced by the images: Frodo needs to reach out his hand to grasp Sam's so that the spectator may know for sure that he chose friendship and freedom above his own self. Somehow, the filmic adaptation changes the configuration of the plot without losing its essence completely.

We insist on the idea that, in the book, the destruction of the Ring comes about mostly by chance; Gollum was so much

---

108. Tolkien, J.R.R. *The Lord of the Rings*. Op. cit., p. 1238.

attached to it that its destruction was almost a certainty. The annihilation of evil, in Tolkien's works, is normally caused by evil itself, and frequently by treason: the Ring distracts Gollum who, hypnotised by the object, trips and falls. Frodo, on the other hand, stayed behind, and the readers' only solace is to know that he did not jump into the precipice with the Ring. But his heroism, as we said, was not shown in the end of the journey, but during it — in his generosity of volunteering several times, in his persistence and strength to carry his burden and, above all, in accepting the challenge to show mercy to Gollum.

The two friends stay together, then, waiting for the eagles to save them — even though they do not know that. Thus, the eucatastrophic ending of this great Tolkienian fairy-story comes about: a happy ending, but not without the marks of heroes' flaws. Sam looks to his friend's mutilated finger and says:

> 'Your poor hand!' he said. 'And I have nothing to bind it with, or comfort it. I would have spared him a whole hand of mine rather. But he's gone now beyond recall, gone for ever.'
> 'Yes,' said Frodo. 'But do you remember Gandalf's words: Even Gollum may have something yet to do? But for him, Sam, I could not have destroyed the Ring. The Quest would have been in vain, even at the bitter end. So let us forgive him! For the Quest is achieved, and now all is over. I am glad you are here with me. Here at the end of all things, Sam.'[109]

With this lesson, Frodo shows not only that evil destroys itself, but also that a good result always comes from not making hasty judgments and from practicing the difficult task of looking for something good in the others, even if such a compassionate attitude may not, at first, seem sensible.

We know that the Hobbits go back home, but with marks — especially Frodo — and new challenges ahead, such as the taking of the Shire by Sharkey and his ruffians. Frodo still has to depart to the Undying Lands to heal his wounds, and his

---

109. Tolkien, J.R.R. *The Lord of the Rings.* Op. cit., pp. 1239-1240.

friends will have to deal with the pain of separation. The Tolkienian eucatastrophe, as we have said, may be fantasy, but it is also realistic: just like his characters demonstrate the belief in the existence of virtuous people, despite their flaws, the happy endings, in Tolkien's legendarium, mirror the victory of Joy in the Gospel, raise awareness to the fact that such a joy is not complete in the physical plane, and that new adventures and challenges are always to come.

Chapter Six

Our Leave-taking

While Merry, Pippin, and Sam are returning to the Shire, after bidding farewell to Gandalf, Bilbo, Frodo, and the Elves in the Grey Havens, they do not exchange a single word, "but each had great comfort in his friends".[1] You and I now finish this book in similar fashion: as in the hero's journey, we are transformed, leaving behind part of our understanding of the world and having learned new lessons. We have, together, felt the strong relation between the bonds of friendship formed during the Quest of the Ring and the idea of consolation and happiness, something that is not exhausted in the pages of the book or in the screens of the cinema but remains in our minds.

This project started with the intention of studying friendship in *The Lord of the Rings*, by J.R.R. Tolkien, and there have been many discoveries along the way that called for more sophisticated analysis. This piece of research grew in complexity and depth and revealed itself gradually. I found out that the studies about friendship, especially in Tolkien's works, are just like his writings: fun and deep, attractive and provocative, full of meanders, subtleties, and ramifications that lead us to brand new branches of knowledge.

Aristotle and Thomas Aquinas showed that, from the philosophical and theological point of view, they are the closest ones to Tolkien's worldview and literary production. We saw, then, that the kind of friendship Aristotle describes as "perfect" is found in individuals who are good in themselves, who regard their friend as another self. Thus, the act of wishing well to the other, which configures benevolence, only becomes friendship

---

1. Tolkien, J.R.R. *The Lord of the Rings*. London: HarperCollins, 2008, p. 1349.

if it is reciprocal. We learned that friendship is intimate and personal, but also communal and politic, as a consequence of dealing with our close fellows.

Friendship is necessary for the chief good of the characters in *The Lord of the Rings*: the destruction of the Ring and the happy ending (eucatastrophe), as well as the presence of friends, were important in the development of each one's trajectory. Besides that, this type of love is a distinguishing feature of those who are close to happiness, because they bring goodness within them and want to share their happiness with the others.

We saw the figure of the hero (or heroes), those whose character is great, and who are capable of practicing benevolence and receiving it back from their companions. However, such heroes are also flawed and mistaken, which favours our identification with them.

As for the movie adaptations, we noticed that understanding the concepts of identification (cosmomorphism) and projection (anthropomorphism) collaborates to the specific analysis of friendship in The Lord of the Ring; moreover, filmic elements awaken, in a special way, the spectators' feelings.

Tolkien's fantasy and the magic of cinema bring relevant elements to guide the readers and the spectators to a Secondary World, where their desire to deal with the animosities of pragmatic life seem to concretise. With fantasy, both in text and movie, the representations of friendship impart identification, empathy, benevolence, and reciprocity between the characters and the audience, whether the reader or the viewer.

By approaching the characters, we are convinced that the relationship Sméagol/Gollum has with himself is a determining factor to his relationship with the other. His double personality, in constant tension, makes hatred and love permanent in his daily life, acting as the driving force of a similar dubious behaviour before the world. The result is that, without completeness, the character cannot love himself and, therefore, cannot love the other. Thus, he cannot be a true friend, and becomes gradually more dependent on the Enemy's Ring, to the extent that he dies for it.

We also learned that the true friendship among characters, especially between Sam and Frodo, is closer to the "perfect" friendship established by Aristotle. On the other hand, all of them are incidental to a greater or lesser extent, due to the human weaknesses of each character, who still had some vices.

However, most members of the Fellowship of the Ring and the free peoples that supported them in the war against Sauron approached virtue during their journey, and approached also perfect friendship, because they wished well to each other. Thus, the heroes of the saga became happier, having friendly relationships as a symptom of and necessity to their happiness and the eucatastrophic outcome.

We observe, moreover, that the good man — the one who has true friendships — is the one with virtue, mercy being the greatest of all virtues (in regard to his relationship with his peers). In Gandalf's presence in Middle-earth, we saw the wisdom of a world uncorrupted by evil, all the more because he was a pupil of the Valië Nienna. It was Gandalf who transmitted to the Ring-bearer, Bilbo Baggins, the lesson of his greatest act of heroism: the capacity of forgiving Gollum for his most terrible flaws. Thus, the virtue acquired by a group of heroes, in spite of their weaknesses, especially courage and mercy, combined with divine providence, the very self-destructive force of evil, and the preponderant role of friendship in the saga of the Ring, lay the groundwork for the desired happy ending in this fairy-story.

The happiness at the end of the saga of the Ring, however, is not complete, because it bears the marks of the defeats suffered by the heroes along their way. It also brings new challenges and the certainty that the concepts of Good and of End, in a physical plane, are not definitive. However, this happy ending relies on friends to come about and, with them, it is celebrated and registered in the story.

With the heroes of *The Lord of the Rings*, we learned that, without friends, virtue would not be conquered and the Quest would not be fulfilled. At last, we come to an end with the consolation of having good companions in our memories and encouraged by the new discoveries that may arise in this endless adventure through Tolkien's universe.

Acknowledgments

To the Great Friend, who inspired and guided me through this project. To His Mother and mine who, like Elbereth, succoured me in the difficult moments.

To J.R.R. Tolkien, for his devotion to his subcreated legendarium, which never ceases to fascinate and surprise.

To the Philosopher, for indicating Virtue to me. To the Doctor Angelicus, for transcending it.

To my dear Peri, for his unconditional support and love in this and many other projects of our lives.

To my parents, for educating me on friendship.

To my generous advisor, Maria Zilda, for believing in me and in the Professor.

To Martin Claret Publishers and the charming Mayara and Carolina, for smiling first to me and to this project.

To Luna Press and Francesca Barbini for welcoming me and giving wings to these words around the world.

To Eduardo Boheme, for his friendly support and courage in the translation.

To professor Diego Klautau, for his good advice and prayer.

To master Ronald Kyrmse, champion of Tolkien's works in Brazil, for his promptitude and kindness.

To Cesar Machado and Sérgio Ramos, from Tolkien Talk Channel, for the time dedicated.

To the University of São Paulo, for being the welcoming house to which I am always back again.

To all my friends who made the journey of my life the happiest possible.

Works cited

AQUINAS, T. *The Summa Theologica*. Translated by the Fathers of the English Dominican province. London: Catholic Way Publishing, 2014.

AQUINO, T. *Suma Teológica*. São Paulo: Edições Loyola, 2012.

ARENDT, Hannah. "On Humanity in Dark Times: Thoughts about Lessing", translated by Clara and Richard Winston, in Arendt, Hannah, *Men in Dark Times*. New York: Harcourt, Brace, 1968 [?].

ARISTOTLE. *The Nicomachean Ethics*, trans. by F. H. Peters, 10 edn. London: Kegan Paul, Trench, Trübner & Co., 1906.

CARPENTER, H. *J.R.R. Tolkien: A Biography*. London: HarperCollins, 2002.

CARVALHAL, T.; COUTINHO, E. (orgs.). *Literatura Comparada — textos fundadores*. Rio de Janeiro: Rocco, 2011.

CASTILLO, Gerardo. *Educar para a amizade*. São Paulo: Quadrante, 1999.

CATUNDA, R.R.B. "Considerações iniciais sobre a eudaimonía e as excelências na *Ética a Nicômaco*". *Polymatheia Revista de Filosofia*, Fortaleza, v.4, n.5, p. 127-144, 2008.

CHESTERTON, G.K. *The Everlasting Man*. London: Hodder & Stoughton Ltd., 1928.

DURIEZ, Colin. *Tolkien and C.S. Lewis: the gift of friendship*. New Jersey: Hidden Spring, 2003.

FOLLAIN, V. "Narrativas em trânsito". *Revista Contracampo*. Niterói, n.21, p. 26-39, 2010.

FORSTER, E.M. *Aspects of the Novel*. New York: RosettaBooks, 2002.

FRITSCH, V.H. "Atravessando Limiares: Simbologias de Passagem no Romance de Fantasia". *Recorte*. Três Corações, n.1, v.11, p. 1-14, jan.-jun. 2014.

GALVÃO, E.V. "Ferramentas conceituais para um estudo da afetividade no cinema". *Interin*. Curitiba, v.15, n.1, p. 163-174, 2013.

GARTH, John. "Sam Gamgee and Tolkien's Batmen", <https://johngarth. wordpress.com/2014/02/13/sam-gamgee-and-tolkiens-batmen/> [Accessed 28 May 2020].

HENRY, Antonin-Marcel. "Introdução", in Aquino, Tomás de. *Suma Teológica*, Livro V. São Paulo: Loyola, 2012

JACOBSEN, L. "The Undefinable Shadowland: A Study of the Complex Question of Dualism in J.R.R. Tolkien's *The Lord of the Rings*". Lund University, Sweden, 1997. <http://tolkiensarda.se/new/alster/shadowland. pdf> [Accessed 24 March, 2020]

JULLIER, L.; MARIE, M. *Lendo as Imagens do Cinema*. São Paulo: Senac, 2009.

KLAUTAU, D.G. 'Do Cinzento ao Branco: o processo de individuação a partir de Gandalf em *O Senhor dos Anéis*'. *Ciberteologia: Revista de Teologia & Cultura*, n.10, p. 10-12, 2007.

_____. "*O Senhor dos Anéis* e o Mal: Corrupção, virtudes e Deus", *Revista Ciências da Religião*, v.6, n.1, p. 90-124, 2008.

KYRMSE, R. *Explicando Tolkien*. São Paulo: Martins Fontes, 2003.

LEGGET, A. *Translating Tolkien: 'The Lord of the Rings' Films as an Imitation, Interpretation, and Emulation of Tolkien's Work*. 2015. Master's thesis. Baylor University, Waco, Texas.

LEWIS, C.S. *The Four Loves*. New York: Harcourt, Brace, 1960.

_____. *God in the Dock*. Michigan/Cambridge: Wm B. Eerdmans Publishing Co., 2014.

LOPES, R.J. *A Árvore de Estórias: uma proposta de tradução para* Tree and Leaf, *de J.R.R. Tolkien*. 2006. Master's thesis, Universidade de São Paulo.

MARTIN, M. *A Linguagem Cinematográfica*. São Paulo: Brasiliense, 2011.

MARTINS FILHO, I.G. *Ética e Ficção de Aristóteles a Tolkien*. São Paulo: Elsevier, 2010.

MONTEIRO, M.R.F. *J.R.R. Tolkien The Lord of the Rings: A Viagem e a Transformação*. 1992. Master's thesis, Universidade Nova de Lisboa.

MORIN, Edgar. *The Cinema, or the Imaginary Man*. Translated by Lorraine Mortimer. Minneapolis, London: University of Minnesota Press, 2005.

NIKOLAJEVA, Maria. *The Rhetoric of Character in Children's Literature*. Lanham, Maryland: The Scarecrow Press, 2003.

PLATO. *The Republic*. Translated by F.M. Cornford. Oxford: at the Clarendon Press, 1955.

RANK, Otto. *Double: A Psychoanalytic Study*, translated by Harry Tucker Jr. Chapel Hill: The University of North Carolina Press, 1971.

ROAS, D. *A Ameaça do Fantástico*. São Paulo: Editora Unesp, 2014.

ROSSET, C. *O Real e seu Duplo: Ensaio sobre a ilusão*. São Paulo: L&PM, 1988.

SALLES, Paulo Emílio Gomes. "A Personagem Cinematográfica", in Candido, A. et al. *A Personagem da Ficção*. São Paulo: Perspectiva, 2007

STAM, R. "Teoria e prática da adaptação: da fidelidade à intertextualidade". *Ilha do Desterro*, Florianópolis, n.51, p. 19-53, jul./dez. 2006.

TODOROV, T. *Introdução à Literatura Fantástica*. São Paulo: Perspectiva, 2004.

TOLKIEN, J.R.R.; CARPENTER, H. (Org.); TOLKIEN, C. (Assist.). *The Letters of J.R.R. Tolkien*. London: HarperCollins, 2006.

TOLKIEN, J.R.R. *The Silmarillion*. London: HarperCollins, 1999.

_____. 'On Fairy-stories', in *Tree and Leaf*. London: HarperCollins, 2001.

_____. *The Hobbit*. London: HarperCollins, 2006.

_____. *The Lord of the Rings*. London: HarperCollins, 2008.

VERNANT, Jean-Pierre. *Myth and Thought among the Greeks*. New York: Zone Books, 2006.

XAVIER, I. (org.). *A Experiência do Cinema*. Rio de Janeiro: Edições Graal, 1983.

YATES, J. *Tolkien as a Writer for Young Adults* <https://www.tolkiensociety. org/app/uploads/2016/11/Tolkien-as-a-Writer-for-Young-Adults.pdf> [Accessed 24 April, 2020].

Secondary reading

AUGUSTINE. *Confissões*. São Paulo: Mundo Cristão, 2013.

ARISTOTLE. *Arte Poética*. São Paulo: Martin Claret, 2004.

ADCOX. J. "Can Fantasy Be Myth? Mythopoeia and *The Lord of the Rings*". <https://goo.gl/YgoSLR> [accessed 22 December 2015].

AGAMBEN, G. *'O que é contemporâneo?' e outros ensaios*. Chapecó: Argos, 2009.

BÍBLIA Sagrada. São Paulo: Ave-Maria, 2009.

BINGEMER, M.C.L.; YUNES, E. (orgs). *Mulheres de Palavra*. São Paulo: Edições Loyola, 2003.

CAMPBELL, J. *O Herói de Mil Faces*. São Paulo: Cultrix/Pensamento, 1997.

CANEVACCI, M. *Antropologia do Cinema*. São Paulo: Brasiliense, 1990.

CANDIDO, A. *Literatura e Sociedade*. Rio de Janeiro: Ouro sobre Azul, 2006.

CARVALHO, L. C. *Jovens Leitores d'O Senhor dos Anéis: produções culturais, saberes e sociabilidades*. 2007. Master's thesis, Universidade Federal do Rio Grande do Sul.

CHESTERTON, G. K. *Considerando Todas as Coisas*. Campinas: Ecclesiae, 2013.

_____. *Ortodoxia*. Campinas: Ecclesiae, 2013.

CHIAMPI, I. *O Realismo Maravilhoso: Forma e Ideologia no Romance Hispano-Americano.* São Paulo: Perspectiva, 1980.

CÍCERO, M.T. *A Amizade.* São Paulo: Escala, 2006.

DROUT, M.D.C. (ed.). J.R.R. *Tolkien Encyclopedia: scholarship and critical assessment.* Nova York: Routledge Taylor & Francis Group, 2007.

ECO, U. *Sobre os Espelhos.* Rio de Janeiro: Nova Fronteira, 1989.

EVARISTO, A.C.F.Q. *O Tempo como Antagonista na Obra 'Somewhere in time', de Richard Matheson.* 2011. Master's thesis. Universidade Presbiteriana Mackenzie, São Paulo.

POMERANTZ, D; LACEY, R. "Top-Earning Dead Celebrities". *Forbes*, October 2009. <https://goo.gl/dTzDuc>. [Accessed 23 june 2016]

FREUD, S. *O Inquietante, in* _____. *Obras Completas.* São Paulo: Companhia das Letras, 2010.

GARTH, J. *Tolkien and the Great War: The Threshold of Middle-earth.* London: HarperCollins, 2003.

HUIZINGA, J. *Homo Ludens.* São Paulo: Perspectiva, 2000.

HUNT, P. (ed.). J.R.R. *Tolkien: The Hobbit and The Lord of The Rings.* Basingstoke: Palgrave Macmillan, 2013.

JAKOBSON, R. *Linguística e Comunicação.* São Paulo: Cultrix, 2007.

LANGER, J. "História e Sociedade nas Sagas Islandesas: perspectivas metodológicas". *Alethéia — Revistas de Estudos Sobre Antiguidade e Medievo*, Bagé, v. 1, 2009.

LIMA, E. "'O trabalho de meu pai teve as vísceras arrancadas' — diz Christopher Tolkien". *Valinor.* <www.valinor.com.br/19340> [Accessed 23 june 2016].

METZ, C. *O Significante e o Imaginário.* Lisboa: Livros Horizonte, 1980.

NADVORNY, M.J. "Narciso e o Auto-ódio". *Espaço Acadêmico*, n.38, july 2004. <https://goo.gl/2uT233>. [Accessed 12 December 2016].

NITRINI, S. *Literatura Comparada: história, teoria e crítica*. São Paulo: Edusp, 1997.

PICHLER, N.A. et al. *A Philia de Aristóteles como uma das Formas de Felicidade*. <http://edgarrogerio.net/arquivos/philia.pdf>. [Accessed 2 February 2016].

PLATÃO. *Lísias*. Brasília: Editora Universidade de Brasília, 1995.

PROPP. V.I. *Morfologia do Conto Maravilhoso*. Rio de Janeiro: Forense-Universitária, 1984.

PURTILL, R.L. *J.R.R. Tolkien: Myth, Morality and Religion*. San Francisco: Ignatius Press, 1984.

RÉROLLE, R. *Tolkien, L'anneau de la Discord*. Le Monde, Paris, july 2005. <https://goo.gl/1fZT7G>. [Accessed 23 June 2016].

RISI, D. *Ator Digital: uma perspectiva de design de personagens*. 2008. Master's thesis, Universidade Católica do Rio de Janeiro.

ROSSI, A.D. "O Senhor dos Anéis: o retorno da épica e o romance histórico no contexto da pós-modernidade". *Revista Iluminart do IFSP*, v.1, n. 3, p. 136-165, December 2009.

SOUZA, L.S. "A Fantasia e o Maravilhoso em O Senhor dos Anéis: a sociedade de Tolkien". *Textura*, Canoas, v. 15, n. 29, p. 62-78, 2013.

SANTAELLA, L. *Por que as Comunicações e as Artes Estão Convergindo?*. São Paulo: Paulus, 2005.

THORDARSON, M.O. *The Theme of Friendship in J.R.R. Tolkien's The Lord of the Rings*. University of Iceland. <https://goo.gl/rtaCW6>. [Accessed 22 December 2015].

TODOROV, T. *Teoria do Símbolo*. São Paulo: Martins Fontes, 1989.

TOLKIEN, J.R.R.; TOLKIEN, Christopher (ed.). *Contos Inacabados*. São Paulo: WMF Martins Fontes, 2014.

TRIANA, B.N.C. "Políticas da Amizade, Poéticas da Alteridade: Uma Análise da Trilogia das Cores de Krzysztof Kieslowski". *II Colóquio da Pós-Graduação em Letras*. <https://goo.gl/7XvnyV> [Accessed 22 December 2015].

WHITE, M. *Tolkien: Uma biografia*. Rio de Janeiro: Imago, 2002.

Audiovisual references

The Lord of the Rings: The Fellowship of the Ring — Extended Version with Appendices. Director: Peter Jackson. Producers: Barrie M. Osborne, Fran Walsh, Peter Jackson, Tim Sanders. Starring: Andy Serkis, Cate Blanchett, Christopher Lee, Elijah Wood, Ian McKellen, Sean Astin and others. Screenplay: Fran Walsh, Peter Jackson, Philippa Boyens. Studio: New Line Cinema/The Saul Zaentz Company/WingNut Films. USA/New Zealand, 2001.

The Lord of the Rings: The Two Towers — Extended Version with Appendices. Director: Peter Jackson. Producers: Barrie M. Osborne, Peter Jackson, Tim Sanders. Starring: Andy Serkis, Cate Blanchett, Christopher Lee, Elijah Wood, Ian McKellen, Sean Astin and others. Screenplay: Frances Walsh, Peter Jackson, Philippa Boyens, Stephen Sinclair. Studio: New Line Cinema/The Saul Zaentz Company/WingNut Films. USA/New Zealand, 2002.

The Lord of the Rings: The Return of the King — Extended Version with Appendices. Director: Peter Jackson. Producers: Barrie M. Osborne, Peter Jackson, Tim Sanders. Starring: Andy Serkis, Cate Blanchett, Christopher Lee, Elijah Wood, Ian McKellen, Sean Astin and others. Screenplay: Frances Walsh, Peter Jackson, Philippa Boyens. Studio: New Line Cinema/ The Saul Zaentz Company/WingNut Films. USA/New Zealand, 2003.

Special materials

BOX Office Mojo's Alphabetical Movie Index. <www.boxofficemojo.com/movies/> [Accessed 15 January 2016].

Dicionário Bíblico. <http://biblia.com.br/dicionario-biblico/> [Accessed 22 December 2015].

Tolkien Talk Channel. <www.youtube.com/Tolkien-Talk> [Accessed 12 December 2016].

Mythgard Institute. <http://mythgard.org/> [Accessed 2 January 2017].

The Tolkien Professor. <https://goo.gl/nPtZtf> [Accessed 2 January 2017].

Tolkien Brasil. <http://tolkienbrasil.com/> [Accessed 12 December 2016] – NO LONGER AVAILABLE.

Tolkien Gateway. <http://tolkiengateway.net/> [Accessed 9 January 2017].

The Encyclopedia of Arda. <www.glyphweb.com/arda> [Accessed 12 December 2016].

The Tolkien Society. <www.tolkiensociety.org/> [Accessed 12 December 2016].

Valinor. <www.valinor.com.br/> [Accessed 12 December 2016].

CPSIA information can be obtained
at www.ICGtesting.com
Printed in the USA
LVHW052009090322
712905LV00020B/1696

9 781913 387938